Praise for
Susan Cameron and
Perfecting Your English Pronunciation

"In my experience, there is no one more insightful and profoundly gifted. Students under her tutelage are radically transformed and earn the right to be competitive in the theater."

Robert Lupone
Director, MFA Program, The New School for Drama,
The New School University

"Susan sets a new standard for excellence in the field of ESL pronunciation, which is available to all who train with her method."

Dr. Pamelia Phillips
Director of Professional Program, CAP21,
and author of *Singing for Dummies*

"Susan worked with my two principal actresses in *Snow Flower and the Secret Fan*. She did accent reduction with them and helped them say their dialogue with more fluency. She was an experienced and creative coach."

Wayne Wang
Film director, *The Joy Luck Club*, *Maid In Manhattan*, and *Smoke*

"This is by far the best instructional video for pronunciation and speech improvement in American English on the market today—her method delivers!"

Bettina Anagnostopoulos
Manager of Corporate Language Training for a global relocation firm

"Whether you are a nonnative English-speaking business person or a native English speaker with an accent seeking career advancement, polishing up your speech with Susan Cameron's technique should be at the top of your to-do list."

Junko Carter
Director of Strategic Alliances, Rhode Island School of Design

"It would have been very difficult to accomplish what I did in my career in the U.S. without Susan Cameron's lessons."

Taro Minami, M.D.
Assistant Professor of Medicine,
Brown University, Alpert Medical School

Perfecting Your

English

Pronunciation

Susan Cameron

New York   Chicago   San Francisco   Lisbon   London   Madrid   Mexico City
Milan   New Delhi   San Juan   Seoul   Singapore   Sydney   Toronto

The McGraw·Hill Companies

For all my students, past, present, and future,
and
in memory of my father, Harold T. MacDonald,
who instilled in me a passion for the English language

2 3 4 5 6 7 8 9 10 11 12 13 14 15   QFR/QFR   1 9 8 7 6 5 4 3 2

ISBN   978-0-07-175017-2 (book, CD, and DVD set)
MHID   0-07-175017-7 (book, CD, and DVD set)

ISBN   978-0-07-174905-3 (book for set)
MHID   0-07-174905-5 (book for set)

e-ISBN   978-0-07-178848-9
e-MHID   0-07-178848-4

Library of Congress Control Number   2010941612

Interior design by Village Bookworks, Inc.

McGraw-Hill books are available at special quantity discounts to use as premiums and sales promotions or for use in corporate training programs. To contact a representative, please e-mail us at bulksales@mcgraw-hill.com.

This book is printed on acid-free paper.

Contents

PART TWO
THE DIFFICULT SOUNDS OF ENGLISH

TWELVE
The vowels of *r* (ɝ and ɚ) 131

THIRTEEN
The vowel ʌ 141

FOURTEEN
The vowel ʊ 155

Acknowledgments

I would like to thank the many people who helped make this book, DVD, and CD set a reality. I am indebted to McGraw-Hill, and especially to my wonderful editor, Holly McGuire, for guiding me through the process of publication. I am eternally grateful to my colleagues, who have taught me so much and who continue to inspire me daily, especially Dr. Pam Phillips, Patricia Fletcher, Deborah Hecht, and Nova Thomas.

For the text of the book, I thank Patricia Fletcher and Nick Cianfrogna for their editing suggestions and input. Thanks, too, to those who helped me in the early writing, especially Sara Wolski, literary consultant extraordinaire; my sister Meg MacDonald, for editing support; Keith Buhl, for lending me his IPA font; Diego Galan, for assistance with the business text in Part Four; and Theodora P. Loukas, for compiling and typing the numerous word lists.

I am grateful to the talented people who helped create the DVD and CDs: Theodora P. Loukas, producer and director; Maggie Mei Lin, filmographer and editor; and Carlos Cano, Chih Hua Yeh, Wayne Liu, Dimitri Letsios, and Angelo Niakas. Special thanks to Anne Goulet, for the "Fred" artwork; Aaron Jodion, for the DVD music; and Eric Maltz, for editing and mixing the CD recordings. I am especially indebted to Theodora P. Loukas and Maggie Mei Lin for making the DVD a reality.

I also thank my wonderful students who appear on the DVD and CDs: Nandita Chandra, Juan Carlos Infante, Vin Kridakorn, Yuki Akashi, Martina Potratz, and Vaishnavi Sharma.

Finally, thanks to all of my past students. You have been my inspiration and my greatest teachers.

Introduction

Fred skipped lunch that Monday afternoon. It wasn't because he was planning to leave the office early for his much anticipated first date with Carla, or that he was saving his appetite for their 7:15 P.M. dinner reservation at the hot new French bistro in the West Village. It wasn't even because of the extra serving of bacon he'd had at breakfast.

Fred skipped lunch because his stomach was churning, his pulse was racing, and his thoughts had begun to jumble. The CEO of Fred's company had flown into the city for a managerial meeting to discuss downsizing at the corporate level, and in an afternoon peppered with presentations, Fred was scheduled to speak first.

Fred was prepared. He was excited about the innovative cost-cutting methods he had devised. His PowerPoint slides were exquisite, his handouts polished, and his presentation of both was well rehearsed. But there was a problem: Fred had to deliver his speech in English, and English wasn't Fred's native tongue. Although Fred's expertise was clear, his pronunciation was not. He worried that if his words were not completely understood, his remarkable contribution would be undervalued.

Sound familiar? If you have picked up this book, it probably does.

Every day, millions of business professionals like you report to jobs dreading the possibility of not being understood. This has nothing to do with talent, skill, or advanced knowledge of the subject; it is because you must speak in the international language of English, and as a nonnative speaker, you have never learned precise pronunciation. This is understandable: When learning English as a second language, most students are taught primarily through reading and writing. What many ESOL classes do not emphasize, however, is that English is a *nonphonetic* language—its spelling patterns often seem to have little resemblance to its pronunciation. At best, this is puzzling; at worst, it can cost talented individuals their jobs.

Consider the words *stop, go,* and *other*; all three are spelled with the letter *o,* but each is pronounced with a different vowel *sound.* Thus, while you may be fluent in English—even a master of vocabulary—*speaking* English clearly and naturally may be difficult. You may also have been influenced by your own ESOL teachers' less-than-perfect pronunciation skills.

Compounding this difficulty is the fact that most languages do not have some of the sounds used in English. You may approximate these sounds, substituting a similar one from your native language, or you may pronounce a word according to the spelling patterns of your native tongue. Even among those speakers of languages that use the Latin alphabet, there is confusion: English has 24 vowel sounds, while most languages of Latin origin have far fewer. In addition, the anatomical placement of English sounds can be especially difficult for natives of Asian cultures, since many vowel and consonant sounds of English are realized much farther forward in the mouth and involve tongue positions not used in Asian languages.

Many Asian ESOL speakers have found success with the *Perfecting Your English Pronunciation* method. In September 1993, I received a telephone call from a diplomat with the Japanese consulate, asking if I might help Prime Minister Morihiro Hosokawa with his English pronunciation: He wanted to be the first Japanese prime minister ever to address the General Assembly of the United Nations in English. Of course, I agreed, and had the honor both to meet and work with the prime minister on his pronunciation and intonation. His English was excellent, and his attention to the nuances of pronunciation exceptional. His address before the General Assembly was, indeed, quite impressive.

Although few of us have to perform on such a public platform, excellent pronunciation is a valuable asset—indeed, a necessity—in any career.

I have had the honor to work with many professionals like you, who, while mastering the skills and knowledge needed to excel in their fields, do not have a clear understanding of the natural sounds and rhythms of English. For example, a brilliant Chinese corporate executive for American Express had been repeatedly overlooked for promotion because his English pronunciation was unclear, and he was often misunderstood in meetings and on conference calls. After we worked with the *Perfecting Your English Pronunciation* method, he understood exactly which sounds were difficult for him and how to correct them—and was able to conduct meetings with ease. Shortly thereafter, he received the promotion he deserved.

I am a strong advocate of diversity in the workplace, and the last thing I want to do is to make all people "sound alike." Many clients have expressed the fear that, in working on accent modification, they will lose their sense of identity, since their speech is a reflection of who they are as individuals and as representatives of their own particular cultures. I completely understand this concern, and I would never advocate nor attempt a homogenization of a global business community. Rather, I am pursuing the opposite result: The goal of the *Perfecting Your English Pronunciation* method is not to reduce the appearance of ethnicity, but to offer individuals the option of speaking clearer Global English (or "Business English," that is, English without the idioms of native speakers). This showcases each person's unique identity and allows expertise to shine through.

I have coached thousands of clients from all over the world—from geographical areas and cultures as diverse as Asia (Japan, India, Korea, China, Hong Kong, Thailand, and Singapore); South America (Venezuela, Argentina, Brazil, Chile, and Peru); Hispanic cultures, such as Puerto Rico, the Dominican Republic, and Mexico; Europe (France, Germany, Switzerland, Portugal, Spain, Italy, Greece, all countries in the British Isles, Russia, and other Eastern European countries, including Hungary, the Czech Republic, Poland, Romania, Albania, Estonia, Turkey, Armenia, Serbia, and Croatia); and many Middle Eastern countries, including Israel and Lebanon. From this large cross section of students, I have identified the 14 difficult sounds and groups of sounds of English pronunciation for all nonnative speakers. And the *Perfecting Your English Pronunciation* method of accent modification has never failed.

Part One introduces the physical placement of sound and the musculature used in articulation. Many other languages rely heavily on the back of the tongue to articulate sounds; by contrast, most sounds in English are formed at the front of the mouth, using the tip of the tongue and the musculature of the lips for consonant placement. You may have trouble with English pronunciation because of excessive tension in the back of your tongue, as well as lack of muscle development in the tip of your tongue and lips. The good news is that this problem is easily overcome by using the exercises described in Chapter One. Think of it as your mouth going to the gym for 10 minutes every day. These exercises are also demonstrated on the accompanying DVD.

Also in Part One, we introduce the system of phonetics, the International Phonetic Alphabet, and provide an overview of the 48 sounds, or phonemes, of the English language.

Part Two forms the core of this book, with one chapter devoted to each of the 14 phonemes and groups of phonemes that you may find difficult to pronounce. Each sound's precise anatomical placement is described in the text, then demonstrated on the DVD. You will need a hand mirror to check for the correct physical placement of sounds; a freestanding mirror is best, since it allows free use of your hands to practice the exercises. The text contains tricks to perfect sound placement, such as putting a finger to your lips to discourage excessive tightening of a vowel.

CD recordings are provided to train your ears in the differentiation of difficult sounds, within both words and sentences. I recommend using an audio recording device (an inexpensive digital recorder or an iPhone or Blackberry application is perfectly suitable) to record your practice sessions; this allows you to compare your own pronunciation with that on the CD recordings.

An additional asset of this book is that it can serve as a mini pronunciation dictionary: Each chapter contains comprehensive word lists—in all, 8,400 of the most commonly used and mispronounced words in English, grouped by sound pattern.

Part Three of *Perfecting Your English Pronunciation* has the "goodies." It addresses the issues of stress, intonation, and operative vs. inoperative words, which collectively create the rhythm of English speech. I say "goodies," because this rhythm often seems to be the most elusive aspect for those struggling with English pronunciation. We focus on stress within words, as well as stress within sentences (also called intonation). Stress within words is often dictated by suffix patterns, which explains the shifting stress in the words *démonstrate, demónstrative,* and *demonstrátion.* The precise rules for syllable stress within words as determined by suffix patterns are explained. Operative and inoperative words are analyzed—those that carry the information in a sentence, as opposed to those that merely provide grammatical structure. Understanding this concept allows you to determine which words are stressed within phrases, clauses, and sentences.

In Part Four, instructions are provided on how to mark and score all your presentations for clearer pronunciation. Sample business presentations are marked for intonation and flagged for difficult sounds. Included are three case studies featuring clients of the *Perfecting Your English Pronunciation* method; these clients dramatically improved their pronunciation using this technique, and the case studies include "before" and "after" recordings of their presentations on the CD.

Welcome to the *Perfecting Your English Pronunciation* method. Let's get started!

PART ONE

GETTING STARTED

ONE

Retraining the articulation muscles

The human body is a glorious, deeply complicated, and vastly explored phenomenon of nature. It also beats the heck out of the anatomy of, say, a snail. Most of us can appreciate this concept through the prism of poets and scientists alike. We speak of the "heart" to describe feelings and emotions that defy scientific explanation; we also (sometimes) listen to doctors who tell us to stop eating fast food if we want our hearts to continue pumping oxygen to all our cells. Poets speak of that which "takes our breath away"; scientists point out that smoking usually does. So we accept that both approaches to the body—mental/emotional health and systemic physical wellness—exist simultaneously and in perfect symmetry.

Why, then, do we not usually accept the fact that language—and the pronunciation of each individual language—is mostly a physical phenomenon, dictated by the dexterity of the articulating muscles that are used in forming speech? I believe this is because speech is a highly personal issue. Indeed, this viewpoint is supported by many idioms in English-speaking cultures: We talk of "having a voice," of "speaking up for ourselves," of "being rendered speechless" versus "shouting to the mountaintops"—all poetic descriptions of the mental and emotional state that predetermines our proclivity for expression.

But when Fred faced his Monday afternoon meeting (see page xv), the last thing on his mind was that, poetically speaking, he had a "lump in his throat" and that nervousness might leave him "tongue-tied." All he knew—or cared about—was that his thoughts were crystal clear and that his speech was not. It was almost, he thought, as he took a sip of water, cleared his throat, and began to speak, that he couldn't *get his mouth to*

3

work fast enough to catch up to the words that were coming out of it. Ironic, yes. But, physiologically speaking, this was exactly what was happening to Fred.

The articulators of speech

Obviously, Fred was upset. He knew he had made so much progress in speaking English—and that doing articulation muscle training felt like he would be "starting from scratch." So, in our session together, I used an analogy. "Suppose you were a marathon runner. You could run 26 miles in less than three hours. And you could sprint a mile in three and a half minutes flat. Your physical condition would be remarkable, and your domination in your field irrefutable, yes?" Fred nodded, and I continued, "Now, because your lower body muscles are in such great shape, I can therefore expect you to walk over to a set of barbells and chest press 300 pounds. Right?"

Fred understood the analogy, even though he was not a marathon runner and had never bench pressed in his life. Different physical disciplines determine different muscle structure. Theoretically, you may be able to squat press exceptionally well, but not excel at chest pressing. So it is with speech: Different languages use the articulation muscles differently. For example, the back of your tongue may be exponentially stronger than the tip of your tongue, based on how your native language utilizes the muscle.

We need to examine the physiology of speech in an objective way. The articulation muscles can be divided into the following categories: the jaw muscle group, the soft palate, the back of the tongue, the tip of the tongue, and the lips. Together, these produce physical speech. Therefore, to learn to pronounce Global English correctly, we have to study—and exercise—all of the articulators that facilitate clear diction.

DVD exercises

The exercises on the accompanying DVD will retrain your articulation muscles in order to master clear Global English speech. Specifically, they focus on the jaw, the soft palate, the back of the tongue, the tip of the tongue, and the lips.

To retrain these muscles and to practice anatomical placement, you must work with a mirror; a freestanding mirror that frees your hands is best. You have to become accustomed to looking inside your mouth at your own articulation muscles, or else you will hinder your progress. For Fred, an inferior performance at an important meeting is far more uncomfortable than 10 minutes in front of a mirror. Some of the placement exercises may require you to feel inside your mouth with your little finger, since retraining the tongue muscle is often realized more readily through tactile placement than through ear training alone. To practice these exercises, first wash your hands, then position yourself in front of the mirror.

These exercises will help you strengthen the articulators in your mouth. Details of individual sound placement follow in later chapters.

The first major muscle that contributes to speech is the jaw muscle group. You may be familiar with the archetype of the "angry young man" that abounds in film—the guy with a clenched, locked jaw, mumbling speech, and finely chiseled bone structure. As enviable as the bone structure might be, the locked jaw is problematic; clear Global English speech requires space in the mouth, and a relaxed jaw makes articulation easier.

Exercises for the jaw

DVD

Articulation
Exercises

*Watch **DVD Articulation Exercises** before attempting the following exercises.* It is important that you perform the retraining exercises correctly. After watching, read the instructions for the jaw exercises, then begin practicing.

1. Release your jaw. Feel it drop open as you part your lips and breathe through your mouth. Feel your tongue resting on the floor of your mouth, with the tip of your tongue resting against your lower teeth, and the back of your tongue down, away from the roof of your mouth.*

---

*This is the base position for the tongue in clear Global English. Practicing this tongue position reduces tongue tension.

Feel how much easier it is to take deep breaths with your jaw relaxed and your tongue resting on the floor of your mouth than it is with your tongue "stuck" to the roof of your mouth and your jaw clenched.

Go back and forth between these two placements—jaw relaxed and breathing through your mouth, then jaw clenched and breathing through your nose. Feel the difference in overall tension between the two.

2. Place your fingers on your jaw muscle. Grit your teeth together and chew. Find the center of your jaw muscle, the point of greatest tension. Now relax your jaw and press the knuckles of your index fingers against the tension point, as hard as you can tolerate. This may feel uncomfortable, since you are breaking up residual tension in the jaw muscle. Hold this position for 15 seconds.

3. Release your hands and feel your jaw drop farther. Take hold of your jaw with both hands and gently pull it downward—but not as far as it can go, pulling the bones out of their joints. You should develop a relaxation in your jaw muscle that allows for a full opening, without joint displacement.

4. Continue moving your jaw up and down, adding sound. Make sure that you are moving your jaw with your hands, not letting your jaw move by itself (that is, not letting your hands "go along for the ride").

5. Press your knuckles against your jaw muscle once again. Practice until you can hold this position for 60 seconds.

6. Shake your jaw out, again adding sound.

These exercises will release your clenched jaw and begin to remedy mumbled speech. Unfortunately, they will not give you a chiseled bone structure.

Exercises for the soft palate

DVD

Articulation
Exercises

*Watch **DVD Articulation Exercises** before attempting the following exercises.* It is important that you perform the retraining exercises correctly. After watching, read the instructions for the soft palate exercises, then begin practicing.

1. Take out your mirror and look inside your mouth. This is a good time to admire yourself and the work of art that is your articulators. After your moment of reverence has passed, it is time to begin exercising the soft palate. Imagine that there is superglue on the tip of your tongue. Glue, or anchor, the tip of your tongue to your lower teeth. Try to yawn, and watch the back of your throat as the soft palate is engaged.

2. Now, form a k sound, then inhale. Look inside your mouth in the mirror. For a full palatal stretch, your soft palate should rise and the back of your tongue should drop down.

3. Practice inhaling and exhaling on a k sound, watching for sharp articulation of the soft palate.

4. With your index finger, hold the front and middle of your tongue in the anchored position (remember the superglue image). Voice a ng-a, ng-a, ng-a sound. Again, watch for agility in the soft palate. (Any tendency to say ng-ga is evidence of tightness in the palate or the back of the tongue.) Repeat this at an increasingly more rapid speed.

5. Practice ng-a on different riffs of rhythm and pitch.

Exercises for the back of the tongue

DVD

Articulation
Exercises

*Watch **DVD Articulation Exercises** before attempting the following exercises.* It is important that you perform the retraining exercises correctly. After watching, read the instructions for the back of the tongue exercises, then begin practicing.

We mentioned earlier how strong the back of your tongue probably is. But all that strength requires a lot of stretching to keep the muscle loose and flexible.

1. Place the tip of your tongue behind your lower teeth. Bulge the back of your tongue forward, stretching it as far as comfort permits. Check in the mirror, making sure that your jaw does not move too.

2. Repeat this motion, adding sound. Notice how much your jaw may tend to move now. With one hand, hold your jaw still while you repeat the exercise.

3. Increase the speed of the exercise, as you maintain the stretch in your tongue.

Exercises for the tip of the tongue

DVD

Articulation
Exercises

*Watch **DVD Articulation Exercises** before attempting the following exercises.* It is important that you perform the retraining exercises correctly. After watching, read the instructions for the tip of the tongue exercises, then begin practicing.

Here come the figurative "chest presses" I mentioned to Fred earlier: strengthening the weaker tongue tip.

1. To focus the tip of your tongue for precision with alveolar consonants (see pages 15–16), point the tip of your tongue toward your little finger. Watching in the mirror, make sure that you do not tighten your jaw or lips.
2. Place your little finger underneath the tip of your tongue and push it up, while resisting with your tongue. Do not use the strength of the back of your tongue to compensate for weakness in the front; this is essentially an isometric exercise for the tip of your tongue. Hold for at least 10 seconds.
3. Relax. Then repeat, pointing your tongue and then pushing up for another 10 seconds.
4. Now let's bring in the artillery. Take a toothpick, and place it against the back of your upper front teeth. Slide it gently upward against your upper teeth, until it touches the gum. Just behind where your gum meets your upper teeth, you'll feel a small bony bump—this is the alveolar ridge. (If the toothpick is pointed, be careful not to jab the gum.) The alveolar consonants (t, d, n, and l) are produced by touching the alveolar ridge with the tip of your tongue. The only sound in English that is made with the tongue touching the toothpick is the *th* sound. Practice making a t sound against the alveolar ridge, making sure that your tongue does not touch the toothpick.
5. Pause the DVD. With the toothpick still in place, make a t sound in time with the ticking of the second hand of a clock, for one minute. Be sure that the t sounds are crisp and made against the alveolar ridge.

Exercises for the lips

DVD
Articulation
Exercises

*Watch **DVD Articulation Exercises** before attempting the following exercises.* It is important that you perform the retraining exercises correctly. After watching, read the instructions for the lip exercises, then begin practicing.

1. Pop your lips forward, using the musculature at the center of both the upper and lower lips. Pause the DVD. Make a popping p sound in time with the ticking of the second hand of a clock, for one minute.
2. Flutter out your lips by relaxing and blowing air lightly through them. Be careful to leave your jaw relaxed, and make sure your tongue is in the base position, at the bottom of your mouth with the tip behind your lower teeth. Hold your hand six inches from your mouth. Aim your breath so that you feel it touching the palm of your hand.
3. Now, "throw a dart" in slow motion, fluttering out your lips. Make sure that you do this all in one breath. (If there is a two-year-old child in the room with you, you will be a huge hit!)
4. Repeat this exercise.

Stop plosive consonants

DVD
Articulation
Exercises

*Watch **DVD Articulation Exercises** before attempting the following exercises.* It is important that you perform the retraining exercises correctly. After watching, read the instructions for the articulation exercises, then begin practicing.

These exercises promote strength and focus in the tip of the tongue. The last two—k and g—also promote flexibility and dexterity of the soft palate and relaxation in the back of the tongue.

1. Practice individual stop plosive consonants as follows.
   a. puh-puh-puh, puh-puh-puh, puh-puh-puh, PAH
   b. buh-buh-buh, buh-buh-buh, bub-buh-buh, BAH
   c. tuh-tuh-tuh, tuh-tuh-tuh, tuh-tuh-tuh, TAH
   d. duh-duh-duh, duh-duh-duh, duh-duh-duh, DAH
   e. kuh-kuh-kuh, kuh-kuh-kuh, kuh-kuh-kuh, KAH
   f. guh-guh-guh, guh-guh-guh, guh-guh-guh, GAH

2. Altogether:
   puh puh PAH, buh buh BAH, tuh tuh TAH,
   duh duh DAH, kuh kuh KAH, guh guh GAH

   It's a catchy chant. Try it again, but this time, all in one breath. Make sure that your jaw remains perfectly still throughout the exercise.

3. For the grand finale, do the exercise forward and backward:
   puh puh PAH, buh buh BAH, tuh tuh TAH, duh duh DAH,
   kuh kuh KAH, guh guh GAH, guh guh GAH, kuh kuh KAH,
   duh duh DAH, tuh tuh TAH, buh buh BAH, puh puh PAH

Congratulations! Your mouth has just completed a full workout at the speech gym.

TWO

The International Phonetic Alphabet

As we saw in the Introduction, the words *stop, go,* and *other* are all spelled with the letter *o,* but they have three different vowel *sounds.* Over the centuries, English has adopted so many words from other languages that its spelling patterns are confusing at best, and at worst they seem arbitrary.

In the late 19th century, a group of British and French linguists invented the International Phonetic Alphabet (IPA), a system that uniquely identifies all of the sounds, or phonemes, used in human languages. Each sound is represented by a single symbol, and conversely, each symbol represents a single sound. The linguists advocated that English spelling be reformed, using a phonetic alphabet to represent the exact pronunciation of words. Unfortunately for us, they lost the battle. Fortunately, they devised a phonetic system by which we can precisely identify pronunciation.

The English language uses 48 sounds: 24 consonants and 24 vowels (including 12 pure vowels, 10 diphthongs, and two triphthongs). A **consonant** is a sound in which the voice, or breath stream, is interrupted or impeded during production. Consonants can be either voiced or voiceless; if the vocal folds vibrate during production, the consonant is voiced, and if they do not vibrate, the consonant is voiceless. All consonants are formed by using two of seven articulators (the lips, the tip of the tongue, the middle of the tongue, the back of the tongue, the alveolar ridge, the hard palate, and the soft palate) either touching or in proximity to each other.

A **vowel**, by contrast, is an uninterrupted voiced sound. For all vowel sounds (with the exception of the vowels, diphthongs, and triphthongs of *r*), the tongue rests on the floor of the mouth, with its tip resting against the lower teeth, and the arch in the tongue determines the phoneme produced.

By now, you have watched the DVD Articulation Exercises and mastered the daily warm-up. Let's move now to the specific articulator placement for consonant and vowel sounds.

Introduction to the consonant sounds

Consonants can be divided into six major categories: stop plosives, nasals, the lateral, fricatives, glides, and affricates. Each of these is named for the way in which the breath stream, or voice, is impeded or interrupted while producing the sound.

Let's review the physiology of the articulators (see the DVD Articulation Exercises and the illustration on page 20). Just behind the upper teeth, where the gums begin, you'll feel a small bony bump. This is called the **alveolar ridge**. Proceeding toward the back, there is the bony roof of the mouth, also known as the **hard palate**. Behind this is a soft fleshy area called the **soft palate**. We explored this in the initial retraining articulation exercises; it is the area of the mouth engaged when yawning and can be most fully sensed when forming a k, g, or ng sound. The **tongue** can be divided into three distinct areas: the back, the middle, and the tip. Other consonant articulators include the **lips** and, less frequently, the **upper teeth**.

As mentioned above, consonants can be either voiceless or voiced. Place your hand on your larynx, or voice box, and say the following sounds: p, then b. Say only the consonant sound—do not add a vowel, as in *puh*. Notice that your vocal folds are not engaged—there is no vibration—for the p sound, but they are engaged for the b. These partner sounds are called **cognate pairs**: Both consonants are produced with the same articulators in the same position, but one of the consonants is voiceless and the other voiced.

Don't worry: While all this information seems very technical, most consonant sounds are intuitively pronounced correctly by English for

Speakers of Other Languages (ESOL) students. Those that may be mispronounced are covered in detail in Part Two (The difficult sounds of English).

The consonants

Most consonants may occur in initial, medial, and final positions in words. **Initial position** is at the beginning of a word, **medial position** is in the middle of a word, and **final position** is at the end of a word. All of these positions are demonstrated in the word examples below; exceptions are noted for certain consonants.

We are now entering the world of phonetics. From now on, we will use the IPA symbol for each sound, rather than the alphabet spelling. IPA symbols are set in sans serif type (for example, b, d, g or *b, d, g*), while spelled words are set in serif type (for example, base, dance, go or *base, dance, go*).

Stop plosives

The breath stream is "stopped," then "exploded" to produce a **stop plosive**. English has six stop plosives.

VOICED PLOSIVE	EXAMPLE WORDS	VOICELESS PLOSIVE	EXAMPLE WORDS
b	base, suburban, cab	p	pay, repeat, stop
d	dance, redeem, need	t	time, intense, past
g	go, regret, flag	k	keep, decrease, desk

Nasals

The sound is released through the nose to produce a **nasal**. English has only three sounds that are nasal. All three are voiced.

VOICED NASAL	EXAMPLE WORDS
m	men, remember, phoneme
n	news, renew, plan
ŋ (ng)	kingdom, thank

Note that ŋ is never used in initial position.

Lateral

The **lateral** is produced laterally, over the sides of the tongue. The tip of the tongue remains in contact with the alveolar ridge, and the sound is always voiced. English has only one lateral.

VOICED LATERAL	EXAMPLE WORDS
l	last, billing, final

Fricatives

A **fricative** is named for the friction created by forcing the breath stream or voice between two articulators. English has nine fricatives.

VOICED FRICATIVE	EXAMPLE WORDS	VOICELESS FRICATIVE	EXAMPLE WORDS
v	victory, invite, save	f	free, affirm, off
ð (th)	this, other, soothe	θ (th)	think, method, math
z	zoo, resume, please	s	see, receive, miss
ʒ (zh)	genre, pleasure, beige	ʃ (sh)	shout, worship, wish
		h	hotel, behind

Note that h is never used in final position.

Glides

The articulators move from one position to another to produce a **glide**. Glides are voiced and are always followed by a vowel sound. English has three glides.

VOICED GLIDE	EXAMPLE WORDS
w	wish, rewind
j (y *or liquid* u)	yesterday, beyond, music
r (*consonant* r)	right, bereft

Note that none of these three consonant sounds, w, j, and r, is ever used in final position.

Affricates

An **affricate** is a combination of a stop plosive and a fricative, blended seamlessly into a single phoneme. English has two affricates.

VOICED AFFRICATE	EXAMPLE WORDS	VOICELESS AFFRICATE	EXAMPLE WORDS
dʒ (j *or* g)	jazz, adjust, age	tʃ (ch)	cheer, achieve, touch

Consonant overview

VOICED CONSONANT	VOICELESS CONSONANT	PLACEMENT AND DESCRIPTION

Stop plosives

b	p	Bilabial (using both lips). The lips come together, then pop apart.
d	t	Alveolar (using the gum ridge behind the upper teeth). The tip of the tongue pops off the alveolar ridge.
g	k	Velar (using the soft palate). The back of the tongue touches the soft palate, then they pop apart.

Nasals

m		Bilabial. The lips come together, the soft palate is lowered, and the sound is released through the nose.
n		Alveolar. The tip of the tongue touches the alveolar ridge, the soft palate is lowered, and the sound is released through the nose.
ŋ		Velar. The back of the tongue touches the soft palate, which is lowered, and the sound is released through the nose.

Continued

Consonant overview (*continued*)

VOICED CONSONANT	VOICELESS CONSONANT	PLACEMENT AND DESCRIPTION
Lateral		
l		Alveolar. The tip of the tongue contacts the alveolar ridge.
Fricatives		
v	f	Labiodental (using the lower lip and the upper teeth). The lower lip contacts the bottom of the upper teeth.
ð	θ	Dental (using the tip of the tongue and the the upper teeth). The tip of the tongue contacts the bottom of the upper teeth.
z	s	Alveolar. The tip of the tongue is in proximity to the alveolar ridge.
ʒ	ʃ	Alveolar. The front of the tongue is in proximity to the alveolar ridge, and the lips are slightly rounded.
	h	Glottal (using the space between the vocal folds). The sound is released through relaxed vocal folds.
Glides		
w		Bilabial. The lips come together and are rounded.
j		Lingual-palatal (using the middle of the tongue and the hard palate). The tip of the tongue is behind the lower teeth, and the middle of the tongue is arched toward the hard palate.
r		Alveolar. The tongue is raised toward the alveolar ridge.
Affricates		
ʤ	ʧ	Alveolar. The tip of the tongue contacts the alveolar ridge, then is pulled back.

Introduction to the vowel sounds

Vowels are uninterrupted, or unimpeded, voiced sounds. Except for the vowels, diphthongs, and triphthongs of *r*, all vowels are made with the tip of the tongue resting against the lower teeth. It is the arch in the front, middle, or back of the tongue that determines the phoneme. *This is important, since most ESOL students have tension in the back of the tongue that causes the tongue muscle to retract (pull back) during vowel articulation.*

Vowels can be divided into three categories: pure vowels, diphthongs, and triphthongs. In the production of a **pure vowel**, the arch in the tongue is fixed throughout the duration of the sound. A **diphthong** is a blend of two pure vowels sounded together as one. A **triphthong** is three vowels sounds blended together as one.

The pure vowel sounds can be categorized as front, middle, and back, named for the arch in the tongue. For a **front vowel**, the front of the tongue is arched; for a **middle vowel**, the middle of the tongue is arched; and for a **back vowel**, the back of the tongue is arched (with the exception of the vowel ɑ, for which the back of the tongue is flat).

The differences between some of these sounds may seem minimal at first, but we will use a tactile approach, so that you can feel each vowel's placement while you simultaneously train your ear. Don't worry if some vowels seem difficult to make at this point. This chapter is intended to be an introduction to the physical placement of vowels according to the arch in the tongue; Part Two explores each of the problematic vowel phonemes in detail, and all the vowel positions are demonstrated on the accompanying DVD.

We are now going to start transcribing entire words using the IPA. Notice how logical the pronunciation seems when viewed through the prism of phonetics. *Note:* When a word contains two or more syllables, one syllable will be stressed more than the others. This syllable is said to carry primary stress and is preceded by the symbol ˈ.

The vowels

English has 12 pure vowels, as shown in the pure vowel overview chart on page 18.

Once you have learned the pure vowels, combining two or three vowels to form a diphthong or triphthong should be easy ('izi). English has 10 diphthongs and two triphthongs, as shown in the charts on page 19.

Pure vowel overview

IPA	SPELLING PATTERNS	EXAMPLE WORDS

Front vowels

i	e, ea, ee, ei, ey, ie, y	be, heat, see, receive, key, chief, happy
		bi, hit, si, rɪ'siv, ki, ʧif, 'hæpi
ɪ	i, y (*except in final position*)	it, hit, miss, since, myth
		ɪt, hɪt, mɪs, sɪns, mɪθ
e	e, ea	jet, mess, dread, head
		ʤet, mes, dred, hed
æ	a	ask, man, thanks, jazz
		æsk, mæn, θæŋks, ʤæz

Middle vowels

ɝ	ear, er, ir, or, ur	rehearsal, person, stir, worst, purpose
		rɪ'hɝsəl, 'pɝsən, stɝ, wɝst, 'pɝpəs
ɚ	er, or (*unstressed syllables*)	singer, mother, actor, comfort
		'sɪŋɚ, 'mʌðɚ, 'æktɚ, 'kʌmfɚt
ə	schwa (*vowel reduction;* see pages 193–195)	the, affront, introduction, dependent
		ðə, ə'frʌnt, ɪntrə'dʌkʃən, dɪ'pendənt
ʌ	o, u	other, love, cup, judge, must
		'ʌðɚ, lʌv, kʌp, ʤʌʤ, mʌst

Back vowels

u	ew, o, oe, oo, u, ue	stew, who, shoe, food, flu, blue
		stu, hu, ʃu, fud, flu, blu
ʊ	o, oo, ou, u	woman, good, book, should, push
		'wʊmən, gʊd, bʊk, ʃʊd, pʊʃ
ɔ	a(l), au, aw, oad, ough	all, August, law, broad, thought
		ɔl, 'ɔgəst, lɔ, brɔd, θɔt
ɑ	a, o (*see Chapter Sixteen*)	father, doctor, stop, body
		'fɑðɚ, 'dɑktɚ, stɑp, 'bɑdi

Diphthong overview

IPA	SPELLING PATTERNS	EXAMPLE WORDS
eɪ̆	a, ai, ay, ei, ey	date, grain, day, freight, weigh, they deɪ̆t, greɪ̆n, deɪ̆, freɪ̆t, weɪ̆, ðeɪ̆
aɪ̆	i, y	time, might, fright, I, sigh, fly taɪ̆m, maɪ̆t, fraɪ̆t, aɪ̆, saɪ̆, flaɪ̆
ɔɪ̆	oi, oy	boil, oil, joy, boy, annoy bɔɪ̆l, ɔɪ̆l, ʤɔɪ̆, bɔɪ̆, ə'nɔɪ̆
oʊ̆	o, oa, ow	go, home, phone, ago, load, know goʊ̆, hoʊ̆m, foʊ̆n, ə'goʊ̆, loʊ̆d, noʊ̆
aʊ̆	ou, ow	about, out, how, now, downtown ə'baʊ̆t, aʊ̆t, haʊ̆, naʊ̆, 'daʊ̆ntaʊ̆n

Diphthongs of *r*

IPA	SPELLING PATTERNS	EXAMPLE WORDS
ɪɚ	ear, eer, ere	clear, fear, steer, cheer, mere klɪɚ, fɪɚ, stɪɚ, ʧɪɚ, mɪɚ
eɚ	air, are	hair, fair, stairs, dare, aware heɚ, feɚ, steɚz, deɚ, ə'weɚ
ʊɚ	oor, our, ure	poor, tour, yours, cure, sure pʊɚ, tʊɚ, jʊɚz, kjʊɚ, ʃʊɚ
ɔɚ	oor, or, ore, our	door, floor, or, more, four, pour dɔɚ, flɔɚ, ɔɚ, mɔɚ, fɔɚ, pɔɚ
ɑɚ	ar	dark, star, far, car, park, stark dɑɚk, stɑɚ, fɑɚ, kɑɚ, pɑɚk, stɑɚk

Triphthong overview

IPA	SPELLING PATTERNS	EXAMPLE WORDS
aɪɚ	ire, yer	fire, retire, tired, buyer, flyer faɪɚ, rɪ'taɪɚ, taɪɚd, baɪɚ, flaɪɚ
aʊɚ	our, ower	our, hour, scour, power, tower aʊɚ, aʊɚ, skaʊɚ, paʊɚ, taʊɚ

Now that you have mastered the articulation retraining exercises and understand how the International Phonetic Alphabet is used to indicate the sounds of English, we can turn to the 14 difficult sounds and groups of sounds of English placement. But first, let's take a look at where the vowel sounds are physically produced in the mouth. We'll use a drawing of Fred's head to map vowel placement.

Fred's head says . . .

This chart of the 12 pure vowels of English shows the arch in the tongue for front, middle, and back vowels. For all vowels except ɝ and ɚ, the tip of the tongue is resting against the lower teeth.

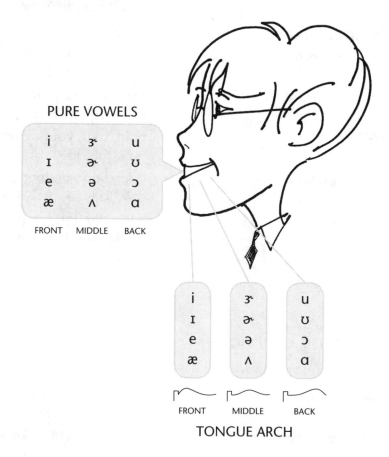

PART TWO

THE DIFFICULT SOUNDS
OF ENGLISH

THREE

The consonant *th* (θ/ð)

Fred was being considered for a new position in his marketing firm: a job that would require frequent oral presentations in English. Fred's boss began to call on him in meetings, and Fred knew that his performance was under scrutiny. Public speaking in English ignited Fred's fears. His mouth would become dry, and he felt his breath grow short and shallow. Fred decided to confide in a colleague. After an especially difficult meeting, he pulled Margaret aside, and told her, in confidence, "I have trouble breeding." Margaret was confused . . .

The *th* sound defined

The *th* sound can be either voiceless (as in the word *thin*) or voiced (as in *then*). The placement is the same, but in the voiceless sound, the vocal folds do not vibrate, and in the voiced sound, they do. These sounds are represented by the phonetic symbols θ (voiceless *th,* as in *thin*) and ð (voiced *th,* as in *then*). Nonnative speakers of English often mispronounce *th* in the following ways: Voiceless *th* (θ) is usually replaced by the consonant t (as in *tin*), and voiced *th* (ð) is usually replaced by d (as in *den*). This is an understandable mistake, since t and d are found in nearly all languages, and the *th* sounds occur almost exclusively in English.

The sounds θ/ð are made very close to t/d, but with a definite difference in tongue placement. For both the t and d consonants, the tip of the

23

tongue touches the alveolar ridge, then flicks off it. When producing a t, the vocal folds do not vibrate; when forming a d, they do. (You may want to refer to the tip of the tongue exercises in Chapter One. Be sure that you are forming t and d off the alveolar ridge, not against the back of your teeth.) θ/ð, on the other hand, are formed with the tip of your tongue touching the bottom of your upper teeth.

Step 1: Feeling the placement of θ/ð

DVD
1

*Turn now to **DVD Track 1**,* where a step-by-step demonstration of the difference between t/d and θ/ð is presented. After you have watched the DVD, read the following description of the sound placement and do the exercises below.

Take out your mirror. Begin by saying the t sound, since you already pronounce this sound correctly. Say the word *tin* several times. Looking in the mirror, begin to become aware of your tongue's placement. Notice that the tip of your tongue touches the alveolar ridge, then flicks quickly off it. Now, lightly place the tip of your tongue against the bottom of your upper teeth. It is not necessary to use the whole front of your tongue. This is the placement for voiceless *th*, θ, as in *thin*. Go back and forth between these two placements: t . . . θ . . . t . . . θ.

Put your fingers against your larynx and say d. Notice that your vocal folds are vibrating, and that the tip of your tongue touches the alveolar ridge, then flicks quickly off it. Now, place the tip of your tongue against the bottom of your upper teeth and allow your vocal folds to vibrate. This is voiced *th*, ð, as in *then*. Alternate between these two placements: d . . . ð . . . d . . . ð.

*Return now to **DVD Track 1**.* Practice the difference in placement between the consonants t/d and θ/ð.

Step 2: Hearing the placement of θ/ð

Using your mirror, look closely inside your mouth. Move your tongue back and forth between the placements of these two pairs of words: *tin*, *thin, tin, thin* and *den, then, den, then.* (Of course, the tip of your tongue will touch the alveolar ridge for the final consonant n.)

Watch in the mirror as you pronounce the pairs of words in the following list. Listen to the consonant sound changes as well, so that you can train your ear to hear the distinction, as well as feel the physiological difference in placement.

t/d	θ/ð
team	theme
tank	thank
tick	thick
tie	thigh
torn	thorn
trash	thrash
tread	thread
tree	three
trust	thrust
tug	thug
dare	there
day	they
dough	though
doze	those
dense	thence

CD
1

Turn now to **CD Track 1**, which features the sound adjustments between t/d and θ/ð. Repeat the pairs of words, while comparing your pronunciation with that on the CD.

Record your own pronunciation, and compare it to the CD track. Repeat this exercise until you feel ready to proceed to the next step.

Step 3: Applying the placement of θ/ð

Following are lists of common English words that contain the *th* sounds. You can practice these sounds by reading these lists aloud. After you have mastered the sounds, advance to the sentences in the next section.

INITIAL ð (VOICED *th*)

that	thence	this
the	there	those
their	therefore	though
them	these	thus
then	they	

MEDIAL ð (VOICED *th*)

another	heathen	slather
blather	heather	slither
bother	hither	smother
brethren	lather	southern
brother	leather	swarthy
clothing	logarithm	together
either	mother	weather
father	neither	whether
fathom	northern	wither
feather	other	within
farther	rather	without
further	rhythm	
gather	scathing	

FINAL ð (VOICED *th*)

bathe	mouth (*verb*)	soothe
blithe	scythe	teethe
breathe	seethe	tithe
lithe	sheathe	with
loath	smooth	

INITIAL θ (VOICELESS *th*)

thank	theory	thick
thatch	therapy	thicket
theater	thermometer	thief
theft	thermos	thigh
theme	thermostat	thimble
theocracy	thesaurus	thin
theology	thesis	thing ►

◄ think   thrash   throttle
third   threat   through
thirst   thread   throughout
thirteen   three   throw
thirty   thresh   thrust
thistle   threshold   thud
thong   thrifty   thug
thorax   thrill   thumb
thorn   thrive   thump
thorough   throat   thunder
thought   throb   Thursday
thousand   throne   thwart
thrall   throng   thyroid

MEDIAL θ (VOICELESS *th*)

aesthetic   brothel   lithography
amethyst   catharsis   marathon
anathema   cathedral   mathematics
anesthesia   catheter   menthol
anthem   catholic   misanthrope
anthology   decathlon   Neanderthal
anthrax   diphtheria   ophthalmology
anthropology   diphthong   orthodox
anthropomorphic   empathy   orthography
antipathy   enthrall   orthopedic
antithesis   enthusiasm   osteopathy
anything   ethereal   parenthesis
apathy   ethic   pathetic
apothecary   ethnic   pithy
arthritis   euthanasia   plethora
arithmetic   gothic   ruthless
atheism   hypothesize   something
athlete   isthmus   stethoscope
authentic   kinesthetic   sympathy
author   lecithin   synthesis
authority   lethal   synthetic
birthday   lethargic   urethra

FINAL θ (VOICELESS *th*)

ba<u>th</u>	fourteen<u>th</u>*	seven<u>th</u>*
benea<u>th</u>	four<u>th</u>*	shea<u>th</u>
ber<u>th</u>	fro<u>th</u>	six<u>th</u>*
bir<u>th</u>	gir<u>th</u>	slo<u>th</u>
boo<u>th</u>	grow<u>th</u>	sou<u>th</u>
bo<u>th</u>	hear<u>th</u>	steal<u>th</u>
bread<u>th</u>	ha<u>th</u>	streng<u>th</u>
brea<u>th</u>	heal<u>th</u>	tee<u>th</u>
bro<u>th</u>	leng<u>th</u>	ten<u>th</u>*
clo<u>th</u>	mir<u>th</u>	tru<u>th</u>
dea<u>th</u>	monoli<u>th</u>	twelf<u>th</u>*
dear<u>th</u>	mo<u>th</u>	twentie<u>th</u>*
dep<u>th</u>	mou<u>th</u> (*noun*)	uncou<u>th</u>
ear<u>th</u>	my<u>th</u>	wid<u>th</u>
eigh<u>th</u>*	nin<u>th</u>*	wor<u>th</u>
fifteen<u>th</u>*	nor<u>th</u>	wrea<u>th</u>
fif<u>th</u>*	oa<u>th</u>	you<u>th</u>
fil<u>th</u>	pa<u>th</u>	
for<u>th</u>	Sabba<u>th</u>	

Sentences: θ/ð

*Turn to **CD Track 2**.* Listen to the recording of the following sentences, then read the sentences aloud. Concentrate on correctly pronouncing the θ/ð sounds, which are marked phonetically.

CD
2

      ð   θ   ð   ð   θ θ   ð θ
1 My bro<u>th</u>er <u>th</u>inks <u>th</u>at <u>th</u>ere is a pa<u>th</u> <u>th</u>rough <u>th</u>e <u>th</u>icket.

      θ   ð   ð   θ   ð   ð   θ
2 Ka<u>th</u>leen's fa<u>th</u>er was from <u>th</u>e nor<u>th</u>; her mo<u>th</u>er was from <u>th</u>e sou<u>th</u>.

      θ   ð ð   θ   ð   ð
3 Be <u>th</u>ankful <u>th</u>at <u>th</u>ere are no <u>th</u>understorms in <u>th</u>e wea<u>th</u>er forecast.

---

*All cardinal numbers except *one, two,* and *three* can be changed to ordinal numbers by adding θ at the end.

4 After surgery, Ma**tth**ew recovered wi**th** **th**orough physical **th**erapy.

5 A sca**th**ing **th**eater review left **Th**addeus see**th**ing.

6 **Th**e **th**ree ru**th**less **th**ieves were **th**warted **th**rough steal**th**y means.

7 Use a **th**esaurus to streng**th**en vocabulary choices **th**roughout your
thesis.

8 An ar**th**ritic knee prevented **th**e a**th**lete from running **th**e mara**th**on.

9 Relax your **th**roat and brea**th**e **th**rough your mou**th**—it's soo**th**ing.

10 Some**th**ing about **th**e uncou**th** you**th** was en**th**ralling.

11 **Th**eoretically, sympa**th**y and empa**th**y produce ca**th**artic results.

12 At **th**ree-**th**irty on **Th**ursday, Timo**th**y will graduate wi**th** a degree
in an**th**ropology.

13 Hea**th**er chose a go**th**ic **th**eme for her twentie**th** bir**th**day party.

14 Hea**th**er's mo**th**er and fa**th**er were not **th**oroughly **th**rilled wi**th** **th**eir
costumes.

15 Is **th**e au**th**or of **th**e logari**th**m an au**th**ority in ma**th**ematics?

16 **Th**eodora received **th**underous applause for her **th**rilling **th**eater
performance.

17 **Th**e clo**th**ing line featured lea**th**er and **th**in synthe**th**ic fabric.

18 Elizabe**th** and Jona**th**an **th**rived wi**th** en**th**usiastic **th**ought.

19 **Th**ousands ga**th**ered in a **th**reatening **th**rong outside **th**e ca**th**edral.

20 Can an argument be bo**th** e**th**ical and pa**th**etic?

Sentences: θ/ð vs. t/d

Turn to CD Track 3. Listen to the recording of the following sentences, then read the sentences aloud. Concentrate on distinguishing between the θ/ð and t/d sounds, which are marked phonetically.

```
    ð      d   ð     t     t d t        ð   d      d  θ
1 The word farther pertains to distance; further describes depth.

    d  d       t t ð       d       d          ð
2 Do deer prefer to teethe on weeds or seeds—or neither?

      θ   d           θ         t        d  ð        t
3 Kathy, do you like Nathan's new tan-colored bathing suit?

      ð   d   t   t t       t       d     ð    ð     θ
4 In the department store, boots were sold in booths on the fourth

      d  θ
and fifth floors.

    ð     θ d  θ        t      d  t  ð       ð
5 The unorthodox thesis was too wordy, but worthy nevertheless.

      d           t    d θ        d t        ð     ð
6 Riding a roller coaster made three-year-old Tammy writhe with

      θ
enthusiasm.

    ð     θ      d ð     t t d   θ      t ð       d
7 The anesthesia allowed the patient to doze throughout the procedure.

    t    t      t      θ      ð      θ    d d      t t
8 Tom's team fought for fourth place in the healthy bread dough contest.

    ð      d  θ  t t ð d   θ   t  ð       t
9 There's a birdbath next to the dense thicket on the nature trail.

    ð  θ    t  ð  d  t θ   d  ð  θ      θ
10 The thorns tore the dainty thread in the thin cloth.

    θ    t   t   t θ    d  ð   t  ð    θ d
11 I thought she taught three days, then took the fourth day off.

      t θ            d ð  t      d  ð  d  ð    θ
12 My cat, Theophilus, followed the trail of bird feathers down the path.

      t t   ð t θ              θ   ð     d t  θ
13 Is it true that therapy can summon both soothing and truthful

    θ    t
thoughts?

      θ  t  t      t  d ð        θ   t      t t
14 Elizabeth trusts her wit and therefore is faithful to her instincts.
```

15 θ   t   θ   θ   tt d ð   ð   t   d
Thrifty Matthew thinks tattered clothing is rather trendy.

16 ð   t   θ   t   t   ð tθ   t
The paucity of thought inherent in that theological argument

        d ð   θ
challenged the faithful.

17 θ   t   θ   θ   dd t d   θ
An authentic synthesis of various theories allowed deft design themes

t θ
to thrive.

18 d   ddð d   θ   ð θ   dθ   d   dθ   ð t
I dreaded the drive through the thick width and breadth of the trash

d
dump.

19 θ   d   θ   t   θ   d θ   t
Theodora, thank you for your spectacularly thorough and thoughtful

     t
contribution!

20   θ   d   d   θ   t   d
You'll be thinner if dinners include healthy vegetables and no

      θ t   t
synthetic substances.

FOUR

The consonant *r*

The *r* sound defined

The consonant *r,* represented by the phonetic symbol r, is almost always mispronounced by nonnative speakers of English. Depending on your native language, you may pronounce r at the back of the throat, or you may trill it off the alveolar ridge. If your native language is Asian, you may pronounce r with tension in the back of your tongue, or the front of your tongue may be touching the roof of the mouth, much like an l.

Step 1: Feeling the placement of *r*

*Turn now to **DVD Tracks 2A** and **2B**,* where a step-by-step demonstration of the placement of r is presented. After you have watched the DVD, read the following description of the sound placement and do the exercises below.

Take out your mirror. Let's examine the position of the tongue in forming the consonant r. Looking in the mirror, place the tip of your tongue against your lower teeth, with your tongue lying flat on the floor of your mouth. Now, arch the middle of your tongue toward the roof of your mouth and point the front of your tongue toward the alveolar ridge. Say r. You'll feel the sides of your tongue touching the inside of your upper teeth.

Again looking in the mirror, watch the movement of your tongue. The tip of your tongue begins against your lower teeth. Now, arch the middle of your tongue toward the hard palate, then lift the front of your tongue toward the alveolar ridge. This is the position for r. Make sure the tip of your tongue isn't touching anywhere inside your mouth.

The most difficult problem you will have with this new, unfamiliar placement is a tendency toward tongue retraction. Because the tip of your tongue isn't touching anywhere inside your mouth, the back of your tongue may tense and retract (pull backward) in order to feel "anchored." As demonstrated on the DVD, place your thumb under your jaw at the base of your tongue. Hold your thumb there firmly as you arch the middle of your tongue and lift the tip. This will prevent your tongue from retracting. You can anchor your tongue by feeling the sides of your tongue lightly touch the inside of the upper back teeth.

Return now to **DVD Tracks 2A and 2B.** Practice the correct placement of the consonant r.

Step 2: Hearing the placement of *r*

Using the mirror, look closely inside your mouth. Move your tongue back and forth between the placements of these two pairs of words: *light, right, light, right.* (Of course, the tip of your tongue will touch the alveolar ridge for the final consonant t.) Notice that the tip of your tongue touches the alveolar ridge for l, but does not touch anywhere in your mouth for the consonant r.

Watch in the mirror as you pronounce the pairs of words in the list below. Listen to the consonant sound changes as well, so that you can train your ear to hear the distinction between l and r, as well as feel the physiological difference in placement.

l	r
lead	read (*both present-tense verbs*)
lie	rye
link	rink
load	road
led	red
lash	rash
low	row
loud	rowdy ►

l	r
◄ lime	rhyme
blink	brink
class	crass
clear	rear
clam	ram
live (*adjective*)	drive
lip	drip

CD
4

Turn now to **CD Track 4**, which features the sound adjustments between l and r. Repeat the pairs of words, while comparing your pronunciation with that on the CD.

Record your own pronunciation, and compare it to the CD track. Repeat this exercise until you feel ready to proceed to the next step.

Step 3: Applying the placement of *r*

Following are lists of common English words that contain the *r* consonant. You can practice this sound by reading these lists aloud. After you have mastered the sound, advance to the sentences in the next section.

INITIAL CONSONANT **r***

brain	bring	cream
brake	British	create
branch	broad	credit
brave	Broadway	crew
bread	broke	crime
break	brother	crisis
breakfast	brought	critic
breath	brown	criticism
brick	brush	crop
bride	crack	cross
bridge	craft	crowd
brief	crash	crown
bright	crazy	cry ►

---

*As the initial sound or in a consonant combination at the beginning of a word.

INITIAL CONSONANT r* (CONTINUED)

◄

draft	grand	price
drag	grant	pride
dramatic	grass	primary
draw	grave	primitive
dream	gray	print
dress	great	prior
drill	Greek	prison
drink	green	private
drive	greet	prize
drop	grew	procedure
drove	grin	process
drug	grip	procure
dry	gross	produce
fraction	ground	production
frame	group	productive
free	growth	professor
freedom	practice	profit
freeze	prayer	profound
freight	preceding	program
French	precious	progress
frequent	precision	project
fresh	prefer	prominent
Friday	prepare	promise
friend	present	promote
frightened	presentation	proof
from	preserve	propaganda
front	president	proper
frontier	press	property
frozen	pressure	proportion
fruit	prestige	propose
grab	presume	prospect
grace	pretty	protect
grade	prevent	protein
graduate	prevention	protest
grain	previous	proud

►

---

*As the initial sound or in a consonant combination at the beginning of a word.

◄ prove

provide

provision

race

radar

radiation

radio

railroad

rain

raise

random

range

rank

rapid

rare

rate

rather

raw

reach

react

read

ready

realistic

rear

reason

receive

recent

recognize

recommendation

record

recreation

red

reduce

refer

refine

reform

refrigerator

refuge

refund

refuse

regard

regime

regiment

region

register

rehabilitation

relationship

relief

remain

remark

remember

remote

remove

render

rent

repair

repeat

report

represent

reputation

require

research

reserve

residence

resist

resource

respect

respond

response

rest

restaurant

restrict

resume

retain

retire

return

reveal

revenue

rhythm

rice

rich

rid

ride

right

rigid

ring

rise

risk

river

road

rock

roll

romantic

roof

room

root

rose

rough

round

route

routine

row

run

rush

Russia

screen

screw

spread

spring

straight

strain

strange

strategic

strategy

stream

street

stress   ►

INITIAL CONSONANT r* (CONTINUED)

◀

stretch	tradition	tremble
strict	traffic	tremendous
strike	tragedy	trend
string	trail	trial
strip	train	tribute
stroke	trait	trim
strong	transfer	trip
struck	transform	triumph
structure	transition	troop
threat	transportation	trouble
through	trap	truck
throughout	travel	trust
thrown	treasury	truth
trace	treat	try
track	treatment	written†
tractor	treaty	wrong†
trade	tree	wrote†

MEDIAL CONSONANT r

abroad	appropriate	authority
abstract	approve	average
accurate	approximate	bureau
across	arbitrary	carriage
address	area	carrier
administration	arise	carry
agree	around	category
America	arouse	century
angry	arrange	character
anniversary	arrest	comparison
apparatus	arrive	compromise
apparent	artery	concentrate
appreciate	astronomy	conference
approach	attractive	confront

▶

---

*As the initial sound or in a consonant combination at the beginning of a word.

†When the *wr* spelling pattern occurs at the beginning of a syllable or word, the *w* is silent.

◄ congregate
congress
considerate
consideration
conspiracy
construction
contemporary
contract
contrary
contrast
contribute
controversy
corporation
correct
correspond
country
courage
curious
current
degree
democratic
demonstrate
depression
describe
description
desperate
destroy
destruction
dictionary
different
direct
direction
director
discovery
discriminate
distraction
distribution
district
doctrine

during
encourage
enterprise
entrance
entry
era
error
Europe
every
experience
experiment
expression
extra
extraordinary
extreme
fabric
factory
favorite
foreign
forest
generation
generous
hatred
hero
history
horizon
hundred
hungry
hurry
hydrogen
impress
improve
increase
incredible
industry
inherit
injury
instruction
instrument

insurance
integration
interest
interference
interior
interpretation
introduce
inventory
January
jury
literary
majority
marine
marriage
maturity
memory
merit
minority
mirror
misconstrue
mystery
narrative
narrow
necessary
numerous
obstruction
opera
operate
operation
orchestra
parade
parents
Paris
period
poetry
reference
sacrifice
satisfactory
secret   ►

MEDIAL CONSONANT r (*CONTINUED*)

secretary	summary	theory
security	superior	thorough
segregate	supreme	tomorrow
separate	surprise	variation
series	surrender	variety
serious	surround	various
sheriff	temperature	very
sorry	temporary	victory
sovereign	terrain	vigorous
spirit	terrible	warrant
story	territory	worry

CONSONANTS r AND l IN THE SAME WORD

agricultural	editorial	military
already	elaborate	milligram
apparently	electric	mineral
approval	empirical	moral
approximately	favorable	natural
April	federal	neutral
barrel	Florida	oral
brilliant	frequently	original
bronchial	general	patrol
Brooklyn	glory	planetary
central	gradually	practical
children	historical	preliminary
chlorine	illustrate	presently
clarity	imperial	primarily
comparable	increasingly	principle
control	industrial	probable
crawl	jewelry	problem
criminal	laboratory	professional
critical	liberal	promptly
crucial	library	proposal
crystal	literally	pulmonary
currently	literature	racial
deliberately	material	radical
delivery	metropolitan	rapidly

◄ rational reliable role
real relieved royal
realize religion rule
really removal salary
recall replace slavery
recently reply strongly
reflect republican struggle
reflection residential temporarily
regardless resolution theoretical
regional respectively traditional
regular responsibility travel
related result trial
relation reveal trouble
relative revolution voluntary
release riffle
relevant ritual

Sentences: *r*

*Turn to **CD Track 5**.* Listen to the recording of the following sentences, then read the sentences aloud. Concentrate on correctly pronouncing the r sound, which is marked phonetically.

     r r   r   r   r   r   r
1 The program director created revenue without raising prices.

       r   r   r   r
2 Will the crowd pay tribute to the courageous hero?

 r   r   r   r   r   r
3 Crime level contributes dramatically to a country's tourism industry.

 r   r   r   r   r
4 Branches of the frozen tree broke off and struck the trailer.

 r   r   r   r   r
5 I really hate driving through rush-hour traffic!

          r r   r   r   r
6 The children rarely rested during spring break.

 r   r r   r   r   r
7 Precision in preparation precedes growth and improvement.

8 Rita and Rick have a travel tradition: a road trip through the
   countryside.

9 The entrepreneur reserved a private room at a reputable restaurant.

10 Rice isn't rich in complete protein, but provides nutrients.

11 Tristan's professor remarked, "Resist propaganda, but promote reform!"

12 Research recommends recreation to rejuvenate and reduce stress.

13 A strategic response can transform trouble into triumph.

14 Andrew was not ready to retire, so he resisted the pressure.

15 The preventative treatment required a rather tricky procedure.

16 Provisions for breakfast included bread and dried fruit.

17 I presume the precious mineral rocks could be crafted into refined
   jewelry.

18 Can the agreement bring relief to the strained relationships?

19 Robert misconstrued his doctrine as correct, superior—and not rigid!

20 Rough terrain surrounded the trail that stretched along the marine.

Sentences: *r* vs. *l*

Turn to CD Track 6. Listen to the recording of the following sentences, then read the sentences aloud. Concentrate on distinguishing between the r and l sounds, which are marked phonetically.

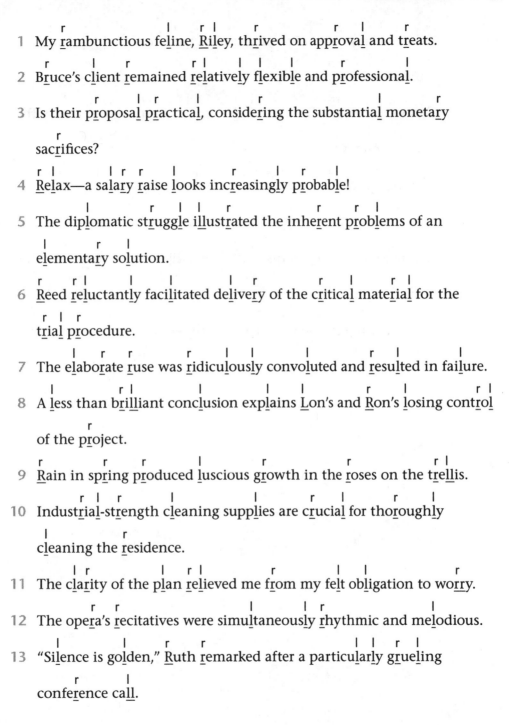

    r   l   r l   r   r   l   r

1 My rambunctious feline, Riley, thrived on approval and treats.

     r   l   r   r l   l   l   l   r   l

2 Bruce's client remained relatively flexible and professional.

       r   l r   l   r   l   r

3 Is their proposal practical, considering the substantial monetary

     r

   sacrifices?

   r l   l r r   l   r   l   r   l

4 Relax—a salary raise looks increasingly probable!

        l   r l l   r   r   r l

5 The diplomatic struggle illustrated the inherent problems of an

   l   r   l

   elementary solution.

   r   r l   l   l   l r   r   l   r l

6 Reed reluctantly facilitated delivery of the critical material for the

   r l r

   trial procedure.

       l   r   r   r   l   l   l   r   l   l

7 The elaborate ruse was ridiculously convoluted and resulted in failure.

      l   r l   l   l   l   r   l   r l

8 A less than brilliant conclusion explains Lon's and Ron's losing control

         r

   of the project.

   r   r   r   l   r   r   r l

9 Rain in spring produced luscious growth in the roses on the trellis.

       r l r   l   l   r   l   r   l

10 Industrial-strength cleaning supplies are crucial for thoroughly

    l   r

   cleaning the residence.

      l r   l   r l   r   l   l   r

11 The clarity of the plan relieved me from my felt obligation to worry.

        r   r   l   l r   l

12 The opera's recitatives were simultaneously rhythmic and melodious.

   l   l   r   r   l l r l

13 "Silence is golden," Ruth remarked after a particularly grueling

     r   l

   conference call.

14 Troubled, angry, and brooding male characters are frequently represented in films.

15 Can we please reach a crystal-clear preliminary agreement by the federal holiday?

16 Empirical proof requires original research through practical planning.

17 Children frequently rely on the natural impulse of role-playing.

18 Harold's relatives loved his blue cheese dip and requested that he bring plenty.

19 Implementing the new resolution resulted in the gradual removal of radical rules.

20 Generally, most people respond favorably to approval and recognition.

FIVE

The consonant *l*

The *l* sound defined

The consonant *l*, represented by the phonetic symbol l, frequently presents a challenge to nonnative speakers of English. Depending on your native language, you may pronounce l too "darkly," with the entire front of your tongue pressed up against the roof of your mouth; this is called velar l. Or your lips may try to pronounce l by rounding, when your tongue doesn't lift. Both placements are incorrect.

Step 1: Feeling the placement of *l*

DVD

3

*Turn now to **DVD Track 3**,* where a step-by-step demonstration of the placement of l is presented. After you have watched the DVD, read the following description of the sound placement and do the exercises below.

Take out your mirror. Let's examine the position of the tongue in forming the consonant l. Looking in the mirror, place the tip of your tongue against your lower teeth, with your tongue lying flat on the floor of your mouth. To form the l correctly, lift your tongue, and place only the tip against the alveolar ridge, just behind your upper teeth. Make sure that your tongue is not touching the back of your upper teeth and that you are using only the tip of your tongue against the alveolar ridge. Now, say l.

Do not round your lips when saying l. Your lips should not move at all during the production of this sound. You can check yourself by placing your index finger against your lips, as demonstrated on the DVD.

Again looking in the mirror, watch the movement of your tongue. The tip begins against your lower teeth. Relax your lips, put only the tip of your tongue against the alveolar ridge, and say l.

*Return now to **DVD Track 3***. Practice the correct placement of the consonant l.

Step 2: Hearing the placement of *l*

Using the mirror, look closely inside your mouth. Begin by making a velar l, whose phonetic symbol is ɫ. Place the entire front of your tongue against the roof of your mouth. Exaggerate by using force as you push your tongue against the hard palate. As you feel the body of your tongue tense, listen for the dark, thick sound that results as you say ɫ.

Now, relax your tongue on the floor of your mouth, and using very little effort, lift the tip to the alveolar ridge, and say *la-la-la-la*. Notice how relaxed this position feels—and how much lighter this l sounds. Go back and forth between these two positions: your tongue tensed against the hard palate (ɫ), then your tongue lightly touching the alveolar ridge: ɫ . . . l . . . ɫ . . . l.

Watch in the mirror as you pronounce the pairs of words in the following list. Listen to the differences between l and ɫ, so that you can train your ear to hear the distinction, as well as feel the physiological difference in placement.

Note: In previous chapters, the correct sound placement for a consonant was contrasted with another frequently substituted phoneme of English. There are no words in English, however, that use a velar ɫ. Therefore, the words in the list below are the same in both columns. The purpose of the exercise is to pronounce each word incorrectly with a velar ɫ, then correctly with an alveolar l. The difference between the two is recorded on the accompanying CD.

ɫ	l
lead	lead (*present-tense verb*)
lie	lie
link	link
load	load ►

ɫ	l
◄ led	led
lash	lash
low	low
loud	loud
lime	lime
blink	blink
class	class
clear	clear
clam	clam
live	live (*adjective*)
lip	lip

*Turn now to **CD Track 7**,* which features the sound adjustments between ɫ and l. Repeat the pairs of words, while comparing your pronunciation with that on the CD.

Record your own pronunciation, and compare it to the CD track. Repeat this exercise until you feel ready to proceed to the next step.

Step 3: Applying the placement of *l*

Following are lists of common English words that contain the l sound. You can practice this sound by reading these lists aloud. After you have mastered the sound, advance to the sentences in the next section.

INITIAL *l**

black	claim	clinical
blame	class	clock
blanket	classic	close
blind	clay	cloth
block	clean	clothes
blonde	clear	cloud
blood	clerk	club
blow	climate	flash
blue	climb	flat ►

*As the initial sound or in a consonant combination at the beginning of a word.

INITIAL l* (CONTINUED)

◀

flax	leader	loan
fled	league	lobby
flesh	lean	locate
flexible	leap	lock
flight	learn	logical
floor	least	London
flow	leather	lonely
flower	leave	long
flu	led	look
fluid	left	loop
flux	leg	loose
fly	legal	lose
glad	legend	loss
glance	legislation	lost
glass	length	loud
label	less	love
lack	lesson	low
ladder	let	loyalty
lady	letter	luck
laid	level	lumber
lake	liberty	lunch
land	lie	lungs
lane	lieutenant	luxury
language	life	placate
languid	lift	place
large	light	placid
last	like	plain
late	limit	plan
Latin	line	plane
latter	linear	planet
laugh	liquid	plant
law	list	plaster
lawyer	listen	plastic
lay	live	plate
lead	load	platform

▶

*As the initial sound or in a consonant combination at the beginning of a word.

◄ play   plus   slip
pleasant   slave   slow
please   sleep   splendid
pleasure   slender   splice
plenty   slide   split
plot   slight
plug   slim

MEDIAL /

ability	below	declaration
absolute	billion	declare
accomplish	biology	decline
alert	bullet	delay
alienation	calculate	delicate
alike	calendar	delight
alive	California	deliver
alliance	capability	development
allies	ceiling	dilemma
allotment	cellar	diplomatic
allow	challenge	discipline
almost	cholesterol	displacement
alone	civilian	display
along	civilization	dollar
also	colleague	early
alter	collection	easily
alternative	college	elect
although	colony	election
altogether	color	element
always	column	eleven
analysis	complain	eliminate
applied	complement	else
Atlantic	complete	elsewhere
available	complicate	elusion
balance	conclude	employ
ballet	conclusion	employee
belief	conflict	English
believe	culture	enliven
belong	daily	envelope	►

MEDIAL l (CONTINUED)

◄ equivalent
establish
evaluation
excellent
exclusive
explain
explicit
exploration
facility
faculty
failure
familiar
family
fellow
follow
formula
gallery
gentleman
golden
guilty
helpless
holiday
holy
ideology
illness
illustration
implicate
inclined
include
influence
intellect
intelligent
involved
island
isolate
July
melody

milligram
million
morality
nevertheless
nuclear
obligation
only
ourselves
outlook
palace
parallel
particular
pathology
peculiar
personality
philosophy
pilot
police
policy
politics
politician
popular
population
possibility
probability
psychology
public
publicity
qualified
quality
salvation
scholar
select
settlement
shelter
shoulder
silence

silver
similar
simultaneous
socialist
soldier
solely
solemn
solid
solution
specialist
spectacular
supplement
supply
surplus
symbolic
talent
technology
telegraph
telephone
television
theology
ugly
ultimate
utility
valley
value
velocity
violence
violet
volume
volunteer
welcome
welfare
wildlife
yellow

FINAL l*

able	channel	example
acceptable	chapel	external
accessible	chemical	fail
actual	child	false
additional	civil	feel
all	clinical	fell
amicable	coal	felt
angel	cold	female
angle	colonel	festival
animal	comfortable	field
annual	commercial	file
appeal	continental	fill
article	continual	film
assemble	control	final
automobile	conventional	financial
ball	cool	fiscal
battle	council	foil
beautiful	couple	fool
bell	cycle	formal
belt	deal	full
Bible	detail	functional
bill	devil	fundamental
binomial	difficult	funeral
bold	disposal	gentle
bottle	double	girl
bowl	doubtful	goal
build	dull	golf
call	economical	guilt
capable	emotional	gulf
capital	entitled	hall
capitol	equal	handle
careful	essential	health
casual	eternal	heel
cattle	eventual	held
cell	evil	hell

───────────

*As the final sound or in a consonant combination at the end of a word.

FINAL l* (CONTINUED)

◄

help	middle	potential
herself	mile	powerful
hill	milk	practical
hold	mill	pull
hole	missile	pupil
hospital	mobile	recall
hotel	model	resolve
hurdle	motel	riffle
ideal	multiple	saddle
impossible	municipal	sail
impulse	muscle	sale
individual	mutual	salt
install	myself	sample
internal	national	scale
international	navel	schedule
interval	noble	school
involve	normal	self
itself	notable	sell
jail	novel	settle
journal	occasional	several
kill	official	shall
little	oil	shell
local	old	signal
mail	pale	single
male	panel	skill
marble	partial	small
martial	particle	smell
marvel	pencil	smile
material	people	social
meal	personal	soil
medical	physical	sold
melt	pile	solve
memorial	pistol	soul
mental	pool	special
metal	possible	spiritual

►

*As the final sound or in a consonant combination at the end of a word.

◄ staple   temple   virtual
   startle   textile   visible
   steal   told   visual
   still   viable   vital
   style   thermal   wall
   substantial tool   wealth
   subtle   total   well
   successful twelve   wheel
   suitable   typical   while
   survival   uncle   whole
   symbol   universal   wild
   table   until   will
   tale   useful   wonderful
   tall   usual   world
   tangible   variable   yield
   technical   vehicle
   tell   verbal

Sentences: *l*

Turn to CD Track 8. Listen to the recording of the following sentences, then read the sentences aloud. Concentrate on correctly pronouncing the *l* sound, which is marked phonetically.

1 I could tell at a glance that Larry learned less from the lesson than Lily.

2 A lack of blame allowed the couple to avoid battle and settle amicably.

3 Full accessibility to the hospital is essential if the clinical trial is

   to be successful.

4 The lighting was functional, but romantic and lovely.

5 Animals are like people—social when handled gently.

6 Linda was startled at the substantial cost of a suitable lawyer.

7 I love Louis Armstrong's recording of "What a Wonderful World."

8 Without a plan, it's a long leap from possible to probable success.

9 Will you fly to Los Angeles for a lengthy holiday?

10 Listen carefully, and eventually you will conclude that Lena is less

than logical.

11 Is it practical for Bill to finalize the commercially viable real estate deal?

12 It's financially impossible to assemble additional automobiles

at the plant.

13 Melinda has gotten slightly slimmer and her clothes look large on her.

14 I longed for the pleasantly cool fall climate by the lake in Lucerne.

15 The employee was labeled as placid, but I believe he's lazy.

16 What languages will develop in civilizations and cultures of the future?

17 Play in life, and health and laughter will follow.

18 The lieutenant's letter listed losses that could easily lead to a costly

lawsuit.

19 Challenging hurdles and difficult dilemmas always enliven Louie.

20 My colleague's complaints complicated the completion of this

particular evaluation.

SIX

The consonant *ng* (ŋ)

Fred was practicing his English pronunciation more often and was beginning to enjoy the sound of his voice. He worked on his *l* placement by vocalizing on *la-la-la-la.* When he saw his colleague Margaret on the elevator, Fred told her of his practice. "Margaret," he confessed, "I'm sinning all the time!"

The ŋ sound defined

The consonant *ng,* represented by the phonetic symbol ŋ, is almost always mispronounced by nonnative speakers of English. This is because the spelling pattern is deceptive: Most individuals pronounce the *n,* followed by a separate *g.* So it was with Fred, who meant to say *singing* instead of *sinning.* But this *ng* spelling pattern in English represents a single phoneme, and its sound is formed in a very different place than that of the consonant *n.* Additionally, this sound is used in the spelling pattern *nk.* When used in an *ng* spelling pattern, only ŋ is sounded. There are some exceptions to this rule, notably when the *ng* spelling is in the root of the word (as in *angle*) and when it occurs in the comparative and superlative forms of an adjective (as in *stronger* and *strongest*). In these instances, the g is sounded in addition to the ŋ phoneme. These exceptions are marked in the following word lists. In an *nk* spelling pattern, the k is always sounded as a separate phoneme: ŋk.

Step 1: Feeling the placement of ŋ

DVD
4

*Turn now to **DVD Track 4**,* where a step-by-step demonstration of the placement of ŋ is presented. After you have watched the DVD, read the following description of the sound placement and do the exercises below.

Take out your mirror. Let's examine the position of the tongue in forming the consonant ŋ. Looking in the mirror, place the tip of your tongue against your lower teeth, with your tongue lying flat on the floor of your mouth. First, we will make an n sound, as a contrast to ŋ. Lift the tip of your tongue, place it against the alveolar ridge, and say n . . . *win*.

Now, let's try ŋ. Place the tip of your tongue against your lower teeth, then raise the back of your tongue until it touches the soft palate, as you do for the consonants k and g. Say k . . . g. Now, lower your tongue to the floor of your mouth again, with the tip of your tongue against your lower teeth. Touch the back of your tongue to the soft palate again, and holding it there, allow the sound to be released through your nose. Say ŋ.

Avoid the tendency to pull your entire tongue backward. You can check yourself by holding the front and middle of your tongue down using the tip of your little finger, as demonstrated on the DVD. Raise only the back of your tongue, and say ŋ . . . *wing*.

*Return now to **DVD Track 4**.* Practice the correct placement of the consonant ŋ.

Step 2: Hearing the placement of ŋ

Using your mirror, look closely inside your mouth. Place the tip of your tongue against the alveolar ridge, and say n. You will hear this sound as both nasal and very forward in the mouth. Now, anchor your tongue against your lower teeth, raise only the back of your tongue until it touches the soft palate, and say ŋ. You will hear a nasal sound here too, but it is realized at the back of the throat. Go back and forth between the two placements: n . . . ŋ . . . n . . . ŋ.

Watch in the mirror as you pronounce the pairs of words in the following lists. Listen to the differences in the consonant sounds, so that you can train your ear to hear the distinction, as well as feel the physiological difference in placement.

n	ŋ
ban	bang
din	ding
fan	fang
sin	sing
ran	rang
pan	pang
kin	king
stun	stung
thin	thing
sun	sung

n	ŋk
ban	bank
clan	clank
fun	funk
in	ink
ran	rank
sin	sink
sun	sunk
tan	tank
thin	think
win	wink

*Turn now to **CD Track 9**,* which features the sound adjustments between n and ŋ. Repeat the pairs of words, while comparing your pronunciation with that on the CD.

Record your own pronunciation, and compare it to the CD track. Repeat this exercise until you feel ready to proceed to the next step.

Step 3: Applying the placement of ŋ

Following are lists of common English words that contain the ŋ sound. You can practice this sound by reading these lists aloud. After you have mastered the sounds, advance to the sentences in the next section.

Note that the ŋ sound does not occur at the beginning of a word in English.

MEDIAL ŋ

anchor	finger*	shingle*
anger*	function	singer
angle*	fungus*	single*
anguish*	gangster	singular*
ankle	hanging	spangle*
anxiety	hunger*	springing
banging	junction	sprinkle
bangle*	language*	stinger
bankrupt	languid*	strangle*
banquet	languish*	stringing
bingo*	linger*	stronger*
blanket	lingo*	strongest*
bronchial	linguist*	swinging
bungalow*	longer*	tangle*
canker	longest*	tango*
cantankerous	manganese*	tincture
conquer	mangle*	tingle*
cranky	mango*	tinkle
crinkle	mingle*	triangle*
dangle*	monkey	trinket
disjunction	punctual	twinkle
distinguish*	punctuation	uncle
donkey	puncture	unction
dungaree*	rancor	vanquish
elongate*	rectangle*	wrangle*
embankment	sanctimonious	Yankee
extinguish*	sanction	

---

*In these words, the *g* is pronounced after the ŋ phoneme.

FINAL ŋ*

-ing (*suffix*)	flank	punk
along	fling	rang
among	flung	rank
anything	flunk	ring
bang	frank	rink
bank	funk	rung
belong	gang	sacrosanct
blank	hang	sang
blink	harangue	sank
boomerang	honk	shrank
bring	hung	shrink
brink	hunk	sing
Bronx	ink	sink
bunk	inning	skunk
chink	instinct	slang
clang	king	sling
clank	kink	slink
cling	larynx	slung
clink	length	song
clothing	lightning	spank
clung	link	sphinx
dank	living	sprang
debunk	long	spring
defunct	lung	sprung
ding	meringue	spunk
diphthong	mink	sting
distinct	monk	stink
drink	nothing	stocking
dunk	oblong	strength
during	pang	string
dwelling	pharynx	strong
evening	plank	strung
everything	plunk	stung
extinct	prolong	succinct
fang	prong	sung

▶

*As the final sound or in a consonant combination at the end of a word.

FINAL ŋ (CONTINUED)

◄ su<u>n</u>k | thro<u>ng</u> | wi<u>ng</u>
swa<u>n</u>k | to<u>ng</u> | wi<u>n</u>k
swi<u>ng</u> | to<u>ng</u>ue | wro<u>ng</u>
ta<u>n</u>k | triphtho<u>ng</u> | ya<u>n</u>k
tha<u>n</u>k | tru<u>n</u>k | you<u>ng</u>
thi<u>ng</u> | twa<u>ng</u> | zi<u>n</u>c
thi<u>n</u>k | weddi<u>ng</u> |

Sentences: ŋ

*Turn to **CD Track 10.*** Listen to the recording of the following sentences, then read the sentences aloud. Concentrate on correctly pronouncing the ŋ sound, which is marked phonetically.

1 A ta<u>ng</u>le of weeds grew alo<u>ng</u> the emba<u>nk</u>ment.
    ŋg   ŋ   ŋk

2 Where is the tip of your to<u>ng</u>ue for all diphtho<u>ng</u>s?
                ŋ   ŋ

3 We sa<u>ng</u> alo<u>ng</u> with a lo<u>ng</u> so<u>ng</u> at the skati<u>ng</u> ri<u>n</u>k.
  ŋ   ŋ   ŋ   ŋ   ŋ   ŋk

4 The you<u>ng</u> company was on the bri<u>n</u>k of ba<u>n</u>kruptcy.
     ŋ   ŋk   ŋk

5 I'm looki<u>ng</u> forward to dini<u>ng</u> at the ba<u>n</u>quet.
     ŋ   ŋ   ŋk

6 Fra<u>n</u>k fu<u>n</u>ctioned well when relyi<u>ng</u> on insti<u>n</u>ct.
  ŋk   ŋk   ŋ   ŋk

7 Li<u>ng</u>er by the fire—the kindli<u>ng</u>'s flame isn't exti<u>ng</u>uished.
  ŋg   ŋ   ŋg

8 We should bri<u>ng</u> hot dri<u>n</u>ks and bla<u>n</u>kets on the outi<u>ng</u>.
        ŋ   ŋk   ŋk   ŋ

9 What is that annoyi<u>ng</u> cla<u>ng</u>i<u>ng</u> and cla<u>n</u>ki<u>ng</u> sound?
          ŋ   ŋ ŋ   ŋk ŋ

10 She was a<u>ng</u>ry when her car tire was pu<u>n</u>ctured.
    ŋg   ŋk

11 Flu<u>n</u>ki<u>ng</u> a crucial test can produce a<u>n</u>xiety.
  ŋk ŋ   ŋ

12 Bring the anchor at a closer angle before sinking it.

13 We mingled with the singers all evening.

14 My uncle owns a housing unit in the Bronx.

15 Slinky and clinging clothing can be flattering.

16 In the spring, turn your clocks forward for daylight savings time.

17 The stars twinkled along the embankment in the evening.

18 There's something soothing about living along the coast.

19 Practicing the English language can prove rewarding.

20 Conquering fears prolongs careers.

Sentences: *ŋ* vs. *n*

*Turn to **CD Track 11**.* Listen to the recording of the following sentences, then read the sentences aloud. Concentrate on distinguishing between the ŋ and n sounds, which are marked phonetically.

1 Fran and Frank were trained in singing harmony.

2 Bring in the next anxious interviewee.

3 Bronchial infections occur during winter months.

4 The Yankees won with a home run in the bottom of the ninth inning.

5 Anything can happen when living by instinct.

6 Dunking for apples during Halloween is an American custom.

       ŋg   n   n   n   n   ŋ

7 My distinguished manager canceled the afternoon meeting.

      n   n   ŋg   ŋ   ŋg

8 Lenny is a genial linguist who speaks a long list of languages.

      n   ŋ   ŋ   n   ŋ   ŋk

9 In creating a strong presence at a meeting, always be punctual.

        ŋ   ŋk ŋ   n n   n n   ŋ

10 Prolonged blinking can indicate that an individual is lying.

       ŋk   n   n   n   ŋk

11 Thank heaven that the machine guns were loaded with blanks!

     ŋk   n   n ŋk   n   n   n   n

12 Monkeys can be cantankerous animals when confined in cages.

        ŋg   n   ŋ   n   ŋk ŋ   n   ŋ

13 My youngest nephew loves splashing and dunking when swimming.

       n   ŋk   ŋ   n   n   ŋk

14 Divide and conquer has long been the plan of vanquishers.

     ŋk   ŋ   n n   n

15 Punctuate the lengthy sentence with a semicolon.

     ŋ   n   n   n   n   ŋ   n

16 Ring in the New Year with champagne and loving company.

     n   ŋ   ŋ n n   ŋk   n   n

17 Ken was wrong to sting Nancy with sanctimonious comments.

     n   ŋ   ŋk   n   ŋ n   ŋk

18 Don't cling to the proverbial anchor when trying not to sink.

     n   ŋg   n   ŋg   ŋ   n

19 My index finger was nearly mangled during the accident.

     ŋ   ŋk ŋ   n   ŋ n   ŋ

20 I long for the distinct ring of a robin's song in spring.

SEVEN

The consonants *b, v,* and *w*

The *b, v,* and *w* sounds defined

The consonants *b, v,* and *w,* represented by the phonetic symbols b, v, and w, are frequently mispronounced by nonnative speakers of English. Depending on the spelling patterns of your native language, you may mispronounce v as either b or w. Another common mistake is to mispronounce w as v.

While this may seem confusing at first, English is actually fairly consistent with spelling patterns for the phonemes b and v, which are represented by the English alphabet letters *b* and *v.*

The w sound may be a little trickier, as it not only represents a *w* spelling in English, but is usually found in the *qu* spelling pattern (phonetically, kw). Sometimes, the *u* spelling in the pattern *gu* is pronounced as w. Additionally, as indicated in Chapter Two (page 14), the w phoneme is always followed by a vowel. Therefore, the spelling of *w* is never a fully lip-rounded consonant phoneme w when it is used at the end of a syllable; instead, the spelling is often accounted for by the use of a vowel or diphthong, as in the words *law, snow,* and *down* (see Chapters Fifteen and Sixteen).

Step 1: Feeling the placement of *b, v,* and *w*

DVD

5

*Turn now to **DVD Track 5,*** where a step-by-step demonstration of the placement of the consonants b, v, and w is presented. After you have watched the DVD, read the following description of the sound placements and do the exercises below.

Take out your mirror. Let's examine the position of the lips and upper teeth in forming the consonants b, v, and w. Looking in the mirror, place the tip of your tongue against your lower teeth, with your tongue resting on the floor of your mouth.

First, let's form a b. Put your lips together, apply a little pressure, pop them forward, and say b . . . *bill.* Now, return your lips to a neutral position. Place your lower lip against the bottom of your upper teeth, keep your upper lip completely still, and say v . . . *village.*

Last, put your upper and lower lips together, round them, and say w . . . *way.* Your upper teeth are not used in forming w.

*Return now to **DVD Track 5.*** Practice the placement of the consonants b, v, and w.

Step 2: Hearing the placement of *b, v,* and *w*

Using your mirror, look closely at your lips and upper teeth. Place the tip of your tongue against your lower teeth. Say b . . . v . . . w, watching your lips and upper teeth for careful placement.

Watch in the mirror as you pronounce the pairs of words in the following lists. Listen to the differences in sounds, so that you can train your ear to hear the distinction, as well as feel the physiological difference in placement.

b	v
ban	van
brain	vain
banish	vanish
bat	vat
bent	vent
broke	evoke

►

b	v
li<u>b</u>erty	li<u>v</u>ery
fi<u>b</u>er	fe<u>v</u>er
du<u>b</u>	do<u>v</u>e
stro<u>b</u>e	stro<u>v</u>e

Turn now to **CD Track 12**, which features the sound adjustments between b and v. Repeat the pairs of words, while comparing your pronunciation with that on the CD.

Record your own pronunciation, and compare it to the CD track.

v	w
<u>v</u>ine	<u>w</u>ine
<u>V</u>in	<u>w</u>in
<u>v</u>est	<u>w</u>est
<u>v</u>eil	<u>w</u>ail
<u>v</u>ault	<u>w</u>all
<u>v</u>egetable	<u>w</u>edge
<u>v</u>erse	<u>w</u>orst
e<u>v</u>il	eq<u>u</u>al
fer<u>v</u>ent	freq<u>u</u>ent
pre<u>v</u>ent	pers<u>u</u>ade
in<u>v</u>ert	in<u>w</u>ard

Turn now to **CD Track 13**, which features the sound adjustments between v and w. Repeat the pairs of words, while comparing your pronunciation with that on the CD.

Record your own pronunciation, and compare it to the CD track. Repeat this exercise until you feel ready to proceed to the next step.

Step 3: Applying the placement of *b, v,* and *w*

Following are lists of common English words that contain the b, v, and w consonants. You can practice these sounds by reading these lists aloud. After you have mastered the sounds, advance to the sentences in the next section.

INITIAL b

babble	bead	biology
baboon	beam	bird
baby	bean	birth
bachelor	bear	bit
back	beast	bite
bacon	beat	bitter
bacteria	beautiful	bizarre
bad	because	black
badge	become	blade
baffle	bed	blame
bag	before	bland
baggage	beg	blank
bait	begin	blanket
bake	below	blast
balance	bend	blaze
balcony	benefactor	bleach
ball	benefit	bleak
ballad	berry	bleed
balloon	beside	bless
ballot	bet	blind
ban	betray	blink
band	better	bliss
bang	between	bloat
bank	beware	blob
banner	bewildered	block
bar	beyond	blood
bark	bias	blossom
barn	bib	blotch
barter	bibliography	blow
base	bicker	blubber
basis	bicycle	blue
basket	big	bluff
batch	bill	blunder
bate	billion	blunt
battery	billow	blur
battle	bin	board
beach	bind	boast

►

◄
boat	brag	brother
body	braid	brought
bogus	brain	brown
boil	brake	bruise
bold	brand	brunch
bolt	brass	brush
bomb	bread	brutal
bone	breadth	bubble
book	break	bucket
boom	breath	bud
boot	breathe	budget
booth	breed	bug
born	breeze	bulb
borrow	bribe	bulge
boss	brick	bulk
botch	bride	bull
both	bridge	bump
bottle	brief	bundle
bought	bright	burden
bounce	brilliant	bus
bound	bring	bush
bow	brochure	busy
bowl	broil	but
box	broke	button
boy	brood	buy
bracelet	brook	buzz
bracket	broom	by

MEDIAL b

-able (*suffix*)	abbey	abject
-ability (*suffix*)	abdicate	able
-ibility (*suffix*)	abdomen	abnormal
-ible (*suffix*)	abduct	aboard
aback	abhor	abolish
abandon	abide	abominable
abate	ability	about

►

MEDIAL b (CONTINUED)

◄

abrasion	attribute	dubious
abroad	audible	durable
abrupt	cabinet	edible
absence	cable	elbow
absolute	caliber	eligible
abstain	capable	embargo
abstract	carbon	embark
absurd	chamber	embarrass
abundance	charitable	embellish
abuse	cobra	emblem
abyss	collaborate	embrace
acceptable	commendable	enable
accessible	comparable	ensemble
accountable	compatible	exacerbate
acrobat	comprehensible	excitable
adaptable	considerable	fabric
admirable	consumable	fabulous
admissible	corruptible	fallible
adorable	credible	feasible
aerobic	crumble	February
affable	cubicle	feeble
albeit	culpable	fiber
album	dabble	flexible
algebra	debate	forbid
ambassador	debilitate	gamble
amber	debit	habit
ambient	debris	hamburger
ambiguous	December	hobby
ambulance	delectable	hospitable
ambush	deliberate	humble
amicable	dependable	illegible
anybody	diabetes	imaginable
applicable	disability	impeccable
approachable	disposable	impossible
arbitrary	disputable	incredible
arbitration	distribute	incumbent
arbor	double	inhabit

►

◄ inhibit

intelligible

irritable

jumble

justifiable

label

labor

labyrinth

liable

liberal

library

limber

lobby

manageable

measurable

memorable

metabolism

miserable

mobile

negligible

negotiable

neighbor

nimble

noble

nobody

notable

number

obese

obey

obfuscate

obligate

oblige

obscene

obsolete

obstruct

obtain

obtrusion

October

ostensible

pebble

penetrable

perishable

phobia

placebo

plausible

pleasurable

pliable

possible

preferable

problem

public

publicity

publish

rabbit

rabble

rabid

ramble

rebate

rebel

regrettable

reimburse

reliable

reprehensible

republic

reputable

respectable

responsible

ribbon

robin

robot

robust

rubric

ruby

rumble

sabotage

satiable

scramble

scribble

sensible

September

shamble

sibling

slumber

somber

stable

stumble

subject

subjective

sublet

subsequent

subside

subsidiary

substance

substitute

subtract

suggestible

suitable

susceptible

syllable

syllabus

symbol

table

tabloid

taboo

tangible

taxable

tolerable

tremble

tribute

trouble

tumble

umbrage

umbrella

zebra

FINAL b*

absorb	job	slob
cab	knob	snob
club	mob	stab
crab	nab	stub
crib	prescribe	sub
cub	probe	tab
curb	rib	transcribe
ebb	rob	tribe
glib	robe	tub
globe	rub	tube
grab	scribe	
jab	scrub	

b AND v IN THE SAME WORD

abbreviate	convertible	variable
above	invincible	vegetable
absolve	irrevocable	venerable
abusive	November	verb
adverb	objective	verbatim
advisable	oblivion	verbiage
ambivalent	observe	verbose
available	obvious	viable
behavior	proverb	vibrant
believe	reverberate	vibrate
beloved	subjective	vocabulary
beverage	subservient	vulnerable
brave	subvert	
brevity	valuable	

INITIAL v†

svelte	vacation	vacillate
vacant	vaccinate	vacuum

►

---

*When the *mb* spelling pattern occurs at the end of a syllable or word, the *b* is silent; examples are *bomb, dumber,* and *lambskin.*

†As the initial sound or in a consonant combination at the beginning of a word.

◄ <u>v</u>agrant

<u>v</u>ague

<u>v</u>ain

<u>v</u>alet

<u>v</u>aliant

<u>v</u>alid

<u>v</u>alley

<u>v</u>alor

<u>v</u>alve

<u>v</u>ampire

<u>v</u>an

<u>v</u>andalize

<u>v</u>ane

<u>v</u>anilla

<u>v</u>anish

<u>v</u>anity

<u>v</u>antage

<u>v</u>apid

<u>v</u>apor

<u>v</u>ariation

<u>v</u>ariety

<u>v</u>arious

<u>v</u>arnish

<u>v</u>arsity

<u>v</u>ary

<u>v</u>ascular

<u>v</u>ase

<u>v</u>ast

<u>v</u>at

<u>v</u>ault

<u>v</u>egetarian

<u>v</u>ehement

<u>v</u>ehicle

<u>v</u>eil

<u>v</u>ein

<u>v</u>elar

<u>v</u>elocity

<u>v</u>elvet

<u>v</u>endor

<u>v</u>eneer

<u>v</u>engeance

<u>v</u>enom

<u>v</u>enerate

<u>v</u>ent

<u>v</u>entilate

<u>v</u>entricle

<u>v</u>enture

<u>v</u>enue

<u>v</u>erdict

<u>v</u>erge

<u>v</u>erify

<u>v</u>ernacular

<u>v</u>erse

<u>v</u>ersion

<u>v</u>ersatile

<u>v</u>ersus

<u>v</u>ertebra

<u>v</u>ertical

<u>v</u>ertigo

<u>v</u>est

<u>v</u>eterinarian

<u>v</u>eto

<u>v</u>ex

<u>v</u>ice

<u>v</u>icinity

<u>v</u>icious

<u>v</u>ictim

<u>v</u>ictory

<u>v</u>ie

<u>v</u>iew

<u>v</u>igor

<u>v</u>ile

<u>v</u>ilify

<u>v</u>illage

<u>v</u>illain

<u>v</u>indicate

<u>v</u>ine

<u>v</u>inaigrette

<u>v</u>intage

<u>v</u>iolate

<u>v</u>iolent

<u>v</u>iolet

<u>v</u>iolin

<u>v</u>irus

<u>v</u>irtue

<u>v</u>isa

<u>v</u>isible

<u>v</u>ision

<u>v</u>isit

<u>v</u>isualize

<u>v</u>ital

<u>v</u>itamin

<u>v</u>ivacious

<u>v</u>ivid

<u>v</u>odka

<u>v</u>ogue

<u>v</u>oice

<u>v</u>oid

<u>v</u>olatile

<u>v</u>olcano

<u>v</u>ulgar

<u>v</u>olley

<u>v</u>oltage

<u>v</u>ulture

<u>v</u>olume

<u>v</u>olunteer

<u>v</u>ortex

<u>v</u>ote

<u>v</u>ouch

<u>v</u>ow

<u>v</u>owel

<u>v</u>oyage

MEDIAL V

-ivity (*suffix*)	convalesce	divulge
activate	convene	drivel
advance	convenient	effervescent
advantage	conventional	elevate
adventure	conversation	eleven
adversary	conversion	endeavor
adverse	convert	envelope
advertise	convey	environment
advise	convict	envision
advocacy	convolute	envy
advocate	convulsion	evacuate
affidavit	cover	evade
aggravate	covet	evaluate
alleviate	crevice	evaporate
alveolar	cultivate	even
anniversary	deliver	evening
anvil	deprivation	event
avalanche	devalue	ever
avarice	devastate	evict
avenge	develop	evidence
avenue	deviate	evil
average	device	eviscerate
aversion	devil	evoke
avert	devious	evolve
aviation	devise	festival
avid	devoid	fever
avoid	devote	flavor
canvas	devour	frivolous
cavalier	disadvantage	galvanize
cavern	discover	government
caviar	diverge	gravity
cavity	diverse	gravy
cavort	divert	harvest
civic	divest	heaven
civilization	divide	heavy
clever	divine	improvise
conservation	divisible	individual
controversy	divorce	innovate ▶

◄ interval

intervene

interview

invade

invent

invert

invest

invigorate

invite

invoice

invoke

ivory

ivy

juvenile

lavender

lavish

level

levity

liver

livid

malevolent

maneuver

maverick

medieval

navigate

navy

never

novel

novice

oval

oven

over

pavement

persevere

pervade

perverse

pivot

poverty

prevail

prevalent

prevent

preview

previous

privacy

privilege

privy

proclivity

provide

provoke

pulverize

ravenous

rejuvenate

renovation

reveal

revenge

revenue

reverence

review

revival

revoke

revulsion

rival

river

saliva

salvage

savage

saver

savvy

scavenge

servant

service

seven

sever

several

severance

severe

shovel

silver

souvenir

sovereign

supervise

television

travel

travesty

trivia

universe

FINAL V

-ative (*suffix*)

-ive (*suffix*)

achieve

active

adaptive

adjective

affirmative

alive

alternative

approve

archive

argumentative

arrive

assertive

attractive

calve

captive

carve

cave

clove

comparative

competitive

concave

conceive   ►

FINAL V (CONTINUED)

◄ connive   give   passive
  consecutive   glove   pejorative
  contemplative grave   positive
  contrive   grieve   preserve
  crave   groove   primitive
  creative   grove   productive
  cumulative   have   receive
  deceive   heave   relative
  decisive   hive   relieve
  declarative   I've   remove
  definitive   imperative   repetitive
  delve   improve   reprieve
  deprive   incisive   resolve
  derisive   indicative   retrieve
  derive   infinitive   revolve
  deserve   initiative   sedative
  disapprove   interrogative selective
  dissolve   intuitive   sensitive
  dive   leave   shave
  dove   live   shelve
  drive   love   shove
  effective   lucrative   sieve
  elective   motive   sleeve
  elusive   move   solve
  evolve   naïve   starve
  executive   native   stove
  figurative   negative   strive
  five   nerve   survive
  forgive   of*   tentative
  fricative   offensive   thrive
  fugitive   olive   you've

*The *f* of the English word *of* is pronounced v.

V AND W IN THE SAME WORD

driveway	twelve	we've
suave	waive	weave
swerve	wave	whatever
swivel	waver	whenever

INITIAL W*

dwarf	swollen	wallet
dwell	swore	wallow
dwindle	thwart	walnut
one	tweak	walrus
suede	tweezers	waltz
suite	twenty	wander
swab	twice	want
swagger	twig	war
swallow	twilight	ward
swamp	twin	wardrobe
swan	twinge	warm
swank	twinkle	warning
swap	twirl	warp
swarthy	twist	warrant
swat	twitch	warrior
sway	twitter	wary
swear	wade	was
sweat	wafer	wash
sweep	waffle	Washington
sweet	wafture	wasn't
swell	wag	wasp
swelter	wage	waste
swift	wagon	watch
swim	waist	water
swindle	wait	watt
swirl	wake	wax
swish	walk	way
switch	wall	we

►

*As the initial sound or in a consonant combination at the beginning of a word.

INITIAL W* (CONTINUED)

◄

weak	when	wine
wealth	whether	wing
weapon	which	wink
wear	while	winter
weary	whimper	wipe
weather	whimsical	wire
web	whine	wisdom
wedding	whip	wish
wedge	whiskers	wisp
Wednesday	whisky	wit
weed	whisper	with
week	whistle	wither
weep	white	witness
weight	whiz	wobble
weird	why	woe
welcome	wick	woke
welfare	wide	wolf
well	widow	women
welt	width	won
went	wield	won't
wept	wife	wonder
were	wig	wool
west	wild	work
wet	will	worn
whale	willow	would
wharf	win	wouldn't
what	wince	wound
wheat	wind	wow
wheel	window	

MEDIAL W

afterward	anyone	await
always	anyway	awake
anguish	anywhere	award

►

*As the initial sound or in a consonant combination at the beginning of a word.

◄ aware
away
awhile
awkward
between
beware
bewildered
clockwise
clockwork
cobweb
crossword
distinguish
elsewhere

entwine
highway
Hollywood
inward
kilowatt
language
languid
languish
linguist
network
nowhere
onward
outward

outworn
penguin
reward
schwa
sidewalk
sideways
somewhat
somewhere
stalwart
subway
upward

w WITH *qu* SPELLING

acquaint
acquiesce
acquire
acquisition
acquit
adequate
antiquate
aquarium
bequeath
colloquial
equal
equate
equator
equipment
equity
equivalent
exquisite
frequent
inquire
inquisitive
kumquat
liquid
liquidate

loquacious
obsequious
quack
quad
quadrant
quadruple
quail
quaint
quake
qualify
quality
qualm
quantity
quarantine
quarrel
quarry
quart
quarter
quartet
quartz
quasi
queasy
queen

quench
query
quest
question
quibble
quick
quiet
quill
quilt
quinine
quintessence
quintuple
quip
quirk
quit
quite
quiver
quixotic
quiz
quota
quotation
request
requiem   ►

W WITH *qu* SPELLING (*CONTINUED*)

◄ require   squalor   squeeze
requisite   squander   squelch
sequel   square   squid
sequence   squash   squint
sequester   squat   squirm
sequin   squawk   squirrel
squabble   squeak   squirt
squad   squeal   tranquil
squalid   squeamish   ubiquitous

Sentences: *b* vs. *v*

CD
14

*Turn to **CD Track 14**.* Listen to the recording of the following sentences, then read the sentences aloud. Concentrate on distinguishing between the b and v sounds, which are marked phonetically.

1 The billionaire served an abundance of caviar at his anniversary party.

2 Beverly is available for babysitting in November.

3 It's commendable when those with abundance volunteer to give back.

4 Take advantage of vibrant, breathtaking views when vacationing.

5 The violin music audibly vibrated above the oboe.

6 Vincent actively advocated having a more collaborative cabinet.

7 Are you capable of absorbing constructive and creative feedback?

8 The movers heaved the heavy boxes into the brownstone.

9 I believe you'll love the new vegetable beverage.

The consonants *b, v,* and *w*   **79**

        v   b   b v   b   b b
10 It's ad**v**isa**b**le to a**bb**re**v**iate the **b**loated **b**i**b**liography.

          b   b   v   v
11 Do you ha**b**itually **b**reathe effecti**v**ely? It's in**v**igorating!

    b b   b   v   v   b
12 **B**ar**b** felt her keen o**b**ser**v**ations made li**v**ing more pleasura**b**le.

          v   b   b   v
13 She o**v**ercooked the **b**acon when **b**roiling it in the o**v**en.

    v   b   b   v b   b   v   v
14 **V**ernon **b**aked **b**atches o**f** **b**iscuits with strawberry preser**v**es and clo**v**e.

       v   b   v   b
15 Alle**v**iate **b**urdens through decisi**v**e and responsi**b**le action.

          v   b   b   v
16 An ad**v**enturous spirit can make one **b**ecome apprecia**b**ly more ali**v**e.

    b v   b   b   v   b
17 **B**re**v**ity is admira**b**le, commenda**b**le, and effecti**v**e in de**b**ates.

    b b   v   v   v   b   b
18 **B**o**b** was conser**v**ative and competi**v**e, al**b**eit hum**b**le.

          v   v   v   b   b
19 The con**v**ersation co**v**ered definiti**v**e strategies for **b**alancing the **b**udget.

        b   b   b   v   v   b
20 The **b**lossoms **b**lew a**b**out in the **v**igorous e**v**ening **b**reeze.

Sentences: *v* vs. *w*

*Turn to **CD Track 15**.* Listen to the recording of the following sentences, then read the sentences aloud. Concentrate on distinguishing between the v and w sounds, which are marked phonetically.

    v   w   w   v   w   v
1 **V**alerie **w**ondered **wh**ether the reno**v**ation plans **w**ould be impro**v**ed.

        w   v   w   v   v
2 She **w**as relie**v**ed to **q**ualify for and recei**v**e an ad**v**ance.

          w   w   v   w v   v
3 Distin**gu**ish bet**w**een con**v**enient equi**v**ocation and real indecisi**v**eness.

       w v   v   v   w   w w   v
4 Dar**w**in **v**oiced a theory o**f** e**v**olution, **wh**ich **w**as **w**idely recei**v**ed.

5 We'll quietly delve into questions before evaluating the controversy.

6 Is there frequently an equal division of work in the development

   division?

7 Wherever one looks in the aquarium, diverse varieties of fish thrive.

8 Quality walking at quick intervals vitalizes vascular health.

9 Which version of your verse do you want to tweak?

10 The travel advisory warned the visitors of high winds.

11 Vin deserves a wage increase when waiving overtime pay.

12 You've been vague about which week you want vacation leave.

13 Witty advertising awards were viewed on television.

14 If delivery were never available, everyone would wonder why.

15 The driver of the vehicle avoided the wet widths of the pavement.

16 Victor thought quality was always advisable over quantity.

17 The waitress at the sidewalk café strives to deliver quick service.

18 Be assertive and avid in your quest to acquire equipment.

19 Think conservatively whenever reviewing which assets to liquidate.

20 Unwise and convoluted conversations can twist language.

EIGHT

The consonant *j* or *g* (ʤ)

The ʤ sound defined

The consonant *j* or soft *g*, represented by the phonetic symbol ʤ, is frequently mispronounced by nonnative speakers of English, since it is confused with the consonant ʒ, as in the word *pleasure*. These sounds are very similar, but with an important distinction in placement. The second element of ʤ is, indeed, ʒ, but it is preceded by the consonant d. Physiologically speaking, the tongue touches the alveolar ridge (to form a d) before pulling back into the ʒ sound.

Step 1: Feeling the placement of ʤ

Turn now to **DVD Track 6,** where a step-by-step demonstration of the placement of ʤ is presented. After you have watched the DVD, read the following description of the sound placement and do the exercises below.

Take out your mirror. Let's examine the position of the tongue in forming the consonant ʤ. Looking in the mirror, place the tip of your tongue against your lower teeth, with your tongue resting flat on the floor of your mouth.

First, we'll form the ʒ sound, since you can form this sound correctly. Say ʒ. Notice that the sides of your tongue are touching the inside of your upper teeth and that the tip of your tongue is pointed toward the alveolar ridge, but not touching it. Say ʒ . . . *massage.*

Next, we'll form the ʤ sound. Raise the tip of your tongue, place it against the alveolar ridge, and say d. Move your tongue backward slightly and feel the sides of your tongue touching the inside of your upper teeth, as you say ʒ. Now, form these two sounds sequentially. Start with the tip of your tongue on the alveolar ridge (for d), then move it slightly backward (for ʒ). Say d . . . ʒ . . . d . . . ʒ.

Finally, we'll combine d and ʒ. Place the tip of your tongue against the alveolar ridge, and pull your tongue backward during the production of the sound. Say ʤ . . . *age*.

Return now to **DVD Track 6.** Practice the correct placement of the consonant ʤ.

Step 2: Hearing the placement of ʤ

Using the mirror, look closely inside your mouth. Place the tip of your tongue against your lower teeth, raise your tongue, and say ʒ. Notice that the sides of your tongue are touching the inside of your upper teeth and that the tip of your tongue is pointed toward the alveolar ridge. Say ʒ. You will hear this sound as long; it will continue as long as your vocal folds are vibrating.

Now, touch the tip of your tongue to the alveolar ridge, form a d sound, then move your tongue slightly backward into ʒ. Combining the two, say ʤ. Listen to the sound produced. This phoneme is much shorter than ʒ, since it is the result of the pressure from the first element (d) releasing into the second element (ʒ).

Watch in the mirror as you pronounce the pairs of words in the list below. Listen to the sound differences as well, so that you can train your ear to hear the distinction, as well as feel the physiological difference in placement.

ʒ	ʤ
sei_z_ure	sie_g_e
trea_s_ure	tru_dg_e
lu_x_urious	lun_g_e
massa_g_e	messa_g_e ►

◄ ʒ	ʤ
plea<u>s</u>ure	ple<u>dg</u>e
<u>g</u>enre	<u>g</u>entle
ca<u>s</u>ual	ca<u>g</u>e
illu<u>si</u>on	ima<u>g</u>ine
le<u>si</u>on	le<u>g</u>ion
bei<u>g</u>e	ba<u>dg</u>e

*Turn now to **CD Track 16**,* which features the sound adjustments between ʒ and ʤ. Repeat the pairs of words, while comparing your pronunciation with that on the CD.

Record your own pronunciation, and compare it to the CD track. Repeat this exercise until you feel ready to proceed to the next step.

Step 3: Applying the placement of ʤ

Following are lists of common English words that contain the ʤ sound. You can practice this sound by reading these lists aloud. After you have mastered the sound, advance to the sentences in the next section.

INITIAL ʤ

<u>g</u>em	<u>g</u>eology	<u>g</u>yroscope
<u>g</u>ender	<u>g</u>eometry	<u>j</u>ab
<u>g</u>ene	<u>g</u>eranium	<u>j</u>ack
<u>g</u>eneral	<u>g</u>erm	<u>j</u>acket
<u>g</u>eneration	<u>g</u>erund	<u>j</u>ade
<u>g</u>eneric	<u>g</u>estate	<u>j</u>agged
<u>g</u>enerous	<u>g</u>esture	<u>j</u>ail
<u>g</u>enesis	<u>g</u>iant	<u>j</u>am
<u>g</u>enetic	<u>g</u>igantic	<u>j</u>angle
<u>g</u>enial	<u>g</u>in	<u>j</u>anitor
<u>g</u>enie	<u>g</u>inger	<u>J</u>anuary
<u>g</u>enius	<u>g</u>inseng	<u>J</u>apan
<u>g</u>entle	<u>g</u>iraffe	<u>j</u>ar
<u>g</u>enuflect	<u>g</u>ym	<u>j</u>argon
<u>g</u>enuine	<u>g</u>ypsy	<u>j</u>aundice
<u>g</u>eography	<u>g</u>yrate	<u>j</u>aunt ►

INITIAL ʤ (CONTINUED)

jaw	joint	juice
jay	jolly	July
jealous	jolt	jumble
jeer	jostle	jump
jelly	jot	junction
jerk	journal	June
jest	journey	jungle
jet	jovial	junior
jiggle	joy	junk
jingle	jubilant	jury
jinx	judge	just
job	judgment	justice
jockey	jug	justification
jog	juggle	juvenile
join	jugular	juxtapose

MEDIAL ʤ

-ology (suffix)	angina	conjure
abject	anthology	contingent
abjure	anthropology	cordial
adjacent	apologize	curmudgeon
adjective	archeology	danger
adjoin	astringent	degenerate
adjourn	astrology	deject
adjudicate	badger	digestion
adjunct	belligerent	digit
adjust	budget	diligent
agency	cajole	dramaturgy
agenda	carcinogen	drudgery
agile	cogent	dungeon
agitate	cogitate	ecology
algae	congeal	education
algebra	congenial	egregious
allegiance	congest	eject
allergy	conjecture	eligible
analogy	conjugate	energy
androgynous	conjunction	engender
angel	conjuncture	engine

◄ enjoy
eulogy
evangelical
exaggerate
fidget
fledgling
fragile
fraudulent
frigid
fugitive
gadget
gorgeous
gradual
graduation
harbinger
homogenous
hydrangea
hydrogen
hygiene
illegible
imagination
immunology
incorrigible
indigenous
ingest
inject
injunction
injure
interject
laryngitis
ledger

legend
legislate
legitimate
lethargy
liturgy
logic
longitude
magenta
magic
magistrate
major
majority
margarine
margin
misogynist
modulate
negligence
nitrogen
objection
objective
original
oxygen
pageant
pajamas
passenger
pejorative
perjure
photogenic
plagiarism
prejudice
procedure

prodigy
project
refugee
regiment
region
register
reject
rejoice
rejuvenate
religion
rigid
scavenger
schedule
sergeant
sojourn
soldier
stingy
strategy
subject
suggest
surgeon
tangerine
tangible
tragedy
trajectory
vegetable
vegetarian
vengeance
vigil
vigilant
Virginia

FINAL ʤ

advantage
age
allege
arrange
assemblage
assuage

avenge
average
baggage
bandage
begrudge
besiege

bridge
budge
bulge
cabbage
cage
carnage ►

FINAL ʤ (CONTINUED)

◄ carriage
cartilage
cartridge
centrifuge
challenge
change
charge
college
converge
cottage
cringe
damage
derange
disparage
diverge
divulge
dodge
dosage
dredge
edge
emerge
engage
estrange
foliage
forage
forge
fringe
fudge
garbage
gauge
hedge
hemorrhage
heritage
hinge
homage
hostage
huge

image
impinge
indulge
infringe
knowledge
large
ledge
lodge
lounge
lozenge
lunge
mange
marriage
merge
message
mortgage
nudge
oblige
orange
page
partridge
patronage
pilgrimage
pillage
pledge
plunge
prestige
privilege
purge
rage
rampage
range
ravage
revenge
ridge
rummage
sacrilege

sage
salvage
sausage
savage
scourge
scrimmage
scrounge
sewage
siege
singe
sledge
sludge
smudge
splurge
stage
storage
strange
submerge
surge
teenage
tinge
trudge
tutelage
twinge
umbrage
urge
usage
verbiage
verge
vestige
village
vintage
voyage
wage
wedge
wreckage

Sentences: ʤ

Turn to **CD Track 17.** Listen to the recording of the following sentences, then read the sentences aloud. Concentrate on correctly pronouncing the ʤ sound, which is marked phonetically.

CD 17

1 Can we adjust the June and July budget on the project?

2 Jill spilled vegetable juice all over her magenta jacket.

3 Our joint agendas addressed both gender and generational subjects.

4 She diligently jotted down notes in her journal throughout the journey.

5 James judged the jargon to be juvenile and objectionable.

6 In January, Gina joined a gym near her job.

7 I was agitated by his negligence and lack of imaginative strategy.

8 Will you study immunology, anthropology, or archaeology in college?

9 The majority must be educated about energy usage and ecology.

10 What is the age range and average wage of the hedge funds' managers?

11 Is this page legitimately original, or was it plagiarized?

12 Don't bring charged and damaging emotional baggage to a marriage.

13 Would you prefer the drudgery of a curmudgeon or the danger

of a degenerate?

14 He rummaged through the ruins and salvaged the ledgers from the

wreckage.

15 John felt rejuvenated by the jovial and congenial passengers.

16 Jennifer's disparaging remark had a damaging effect on the jury.

17 The sergeant enjoyed geology, geography, geometry, and algebra.

18 My allergic reaction to the foliage verged on laryngitis.

19 Is justice always objective, logical, and genuine?

20 Jeremiah objected to procedure based on conjecture and demanded

an apology.

Sentences: ʤ vs. ʒ

*Turn to **CD Track 18**.* Listen to the recording of the following sentences, then read the sentences aloud. Concentrate on distinguishing between the ʤ and ʒ sounds, which are marked phonetically.

1 It's a pleasure to digest an argument that is logical and cogent.

2 Who can measure the damage of an egregious error?

3 After the seizure, the surgeon's vision gradually worsened.

4 Take advantage of leisure time, and indulge lethargic impulses.

5 I treasure an ability to visualize challenge as pleasurable.

6 Is the dress code at the lodge's lounge usually casual?

7 Georgia's teenage protégé was a genius and a joy to teach.

8 Occasionally, Jen exaggerated her knowledge of a subject.

9 The merger gave the illusion that they had forged a prestigious new

agency.

10 Jasper thought that the sale of the loft was contingent on persuasion through badgering.

11 Splurge on a massage and a luxurious, but energizing, range of activities.

12 The sergeant had his soldiers wear camouflage during the siege.

13 Joining forces involved collusion with fraudulent measures.

14 Take advantage of the festival and enjoy your favorite film genre.

15 Madge's teenagers usually felt obliged to accompany her on religious outings.

16 I take umbrage at Jessica's urge to feign prestige through excessive verbiage.

17 The vintage clothing line included gorgeous rouge lingerie and treasured jewelry.

18 I envisioned that my mortgage rate would surge and tried to adjust my budget.

19 You can sabotage your energy by eating carcinogens while on a hectic schedule.

20 Allusions to eligible singles abounded in the graduate student's journal.

NINE

The vowel ɪ

Fred was excited: He had been flown into New York City to interview for a highly coveted position at a large securities firm. During the taxi ride from the airport, he saw the city in its dizzying splendor—from skyscrapers to street vendors. Fred could picture himself living here as a true New Yorker, and he wanted to convey that to his potential boss. As he shook the CEO's hand, he announced passionately, "I want to leave here! Now!" The CEO was confused . . .

The ɪ sound defined

For nonnative speakers of English, the short *i* sound, represented by the phonetic symbol ɪ (as in *him*), is often confused with the vowel i (as in *he*). This is an understandable mistake, since i is used by nearly all languages and ɪ is used almost exclusively by English. These two different vowel sounds are made very close to each other, but with a definite difference in tongue placement.

Both i and ɪ are front vowels: The tip of the tongue is resting against the lower teeth and it is the arch in the front of the tongue that determines the vowels' sounds. The difference in the arch is minuscule—about one-eighth of an inch.

Correcting the i vs. ɪ vowel substitution is easy, once you learn the difference in tongue placement. It is also easy to recognize which of the two is used, based on the spelling patterns of each vowel.

The easily recognized i sound in English is spelled with *e, ea, ee, ei,* and *ie,* as in the words *be, eat, see, receive,* and *chief.* Final *y* in English words use the i sound, as in *happy* and *country.* The ɪ sound is almost always spelled with *i,* as in the words *in, with,* and *his,* or with medial *y,* as in *myth* and *syllable.*

Since most languages other than English pronounce *i* as i, its pronunciation as ɪ may be unfamiliar to you. As we saw in the unfortunate story above, Fred pronounced *live* as if it were *leave.* Similarly, you may think *is* is pronounced as *ease,* and *sit* as *seat,* but this is incorrect.

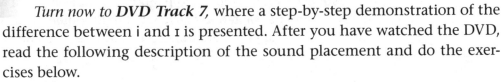

Step 1: Feeling the placement of ɪ

DVD

7

*Turn now to **DVD Track 7**,* where a step-by-step demonstration of the difference between i and ɪ is presented. After you have watched the DVD, read the following description of the sound placement and do the exercises below.

Take out your mirror. Begin by saying the i sound, since you already pronounce this sound correctly. Say the word *he* several times. Looking in the mirror, become aware of your tongue's placement. Notice that the tip of your tongue is resting against your lower teeth and that the front of your tongue is arched forward. You can check yourself by placing the tip of your little finger on the top edge of your lower teeth, as demonstrated on the DVD. Feel the arch in the front of your tongue as it contacts your finger when you say *he.*

Return your tongue to its resting position, with the tip of your tongue against your lower teeth, but with the body of your tongue lying flat on the floor of your mouth. Say the word *he* again, freezing on the vowel. Once again, you will feel the arch of your tongue contact the tip of your finger.

Now, drop the arch of your tongue backward about one-eighth of an inch, leaving the tip of your tongue against your lower teeth. This is the placement of the vowel ɪ, as in the word *him.* Go back and forth between these two placements: i . . . ɪ . . . i . . . ɪ.

*Return now to **DVD Track 7.*** Practice the difference in placement between the sounds i and ɪ.

Step 2: Hearing the placement of ɪ

Using the mirror, look closely inside your mouth. Move your tongue back and forth between the placements of these two words: *he . . . him . . . he . . . him . . . he . . . him . . . he . . . him.* (Of course, your lips will come together for the consonant m.)

Watch in the mirror as you pronounce the pairs of words in the following list. Listen to the differences between i and ɪ, so that you can train your ear to hear the distinction, as well as feel the physiological difference in placement.

i	ɪ
be	bit
peel	pill
seat	sit
tea	tin
keep	king
meal	mill
eat	it
cheap	chip
these	this
reap	rip
feel	fill
heat	hit
feet	fit
key	kill
neat	knit

*Turn now to **CD Track 19,*** which features the sound adjustments between i and ɪ. Repeat the pairs of words, while comparing your pronunciation with that on the CD.

Record your own pronunciation, and compare it to the CD track. Repeat this exercise until you feel ready to proceed to the next step.

Step 3: Applying the placement of ɪ

Following are lists of common English words that contain the ɪ sound. You can practice this sound by reading these lists aloud. The lists are quite extensive, since ɪ is the second most common vowel sound in English. After you have mastered the sound, advance to the sentences in the next section.

ɪ IN ONE-SYLLABLE WORDS

-ing (*suffix*)	gift	miss
mis- (*prefix*)	give	mist
been	grim	mix
bid	grin	pick
big	grip	pill
bills	guilt	pin
bit	hill	pink
brick	him	pit
bridge	hip	pitch
bring	his	prince
brisk	hit	print
build	if	quick
chill	ill	quit
chin	in	ribs
chip	inch	rich
did	is	rid
dip	it	ring
dish	kid	rip
disk	kill	risk
drill	king	script
drink	kiss	ship
drip	lick	sick
fifth	lid	sin
fig	lift	since
fill	limb	sink
film	lint	sing
fish	lip	sit
fist	list	six
fit	live (*verb*)	skill
fix	milk	skin
flip	mill	slid

►

◄ slim   strip   tip
slip   swift   trim
split   swim   trip
spill   swing   which
spring   switch   whip
squid   thick   will
stick   thin   win
stiff   thing   wind (*noun*)
still   think   wing
sting   this   wish
strict   till   wit
string   tin   with

I IN TWO-SYLLABLE WORDS

acting   brilliant   cleaning
active   bringing   clinic
adding   British   closing
admit   building   clothing
artist   burning   coming
asking   business†   conflict
assist   bustling   consists
basic   busy   convict
basis   buying   convince
bearing   cabin   cooking
begin*   calling   cooling
being   captive   cousin
Berlin   ceiling   credit
bigger   changing   crisis
billboard   charming   critic
billing   chicken   crossing
billion   children   cutting
binding   Christmas   dealing
bitter   chronic   didn't
bizarre   city   dinner
breaking   civil   direct
breathing   classic   discharge   ►

*This word has the letter *e* in an unstressed first syllable; the *e* is pronounced ɪ.
†This word has the letter *e* in a suffix; the *e* is pronounced ɪ (see Appendix A).

ɪ IN TWO-SYLLABLE WORDS (*CONTINUED*)

◄

disease	fifteen	hearing
disgusts	fifty	heating
display	fighting	helping
distance	figure	himself
distinct	filthy	hither
district	finger	hitting
disturb	finish	holding
divine	firing	hoping
divorce	fiscal	horrid
doctrine	fishing	hospice
doing	fitting	hunting
drawing	flicker	ignore
dressing	fluid	image†
dripping	flying	impact
driven	forbid	imposed
drying	foreign	impress
during	forgive	improve
dying	forming	impulse
earnings	friendship	inclined
eating	fulfill	include
edit	furnish	income
ending	getting	increase
engine	giddy	indeed
English	giving	index
ethics	glitter	indoors
exist*	going	infer
exit	granite	inflict
fabric	graphic	inform
facing	growing	injure
falling	guilty	inner
famine	guitar	input
feeding	habit	insects
feeling	having	inside
fiction	heading	insight

►

*This word has the letter *e* in an unstressed first syllable; the *e* is pronounced ɪ.
†This word has the letter *a* in a suffix; the *a* is pronounced ɪ (see Appendix A).

◄ insist
   inspired
   install
   instance
   instead
   insult
   insure
   intense
   interest*
   intern
   into
   intrigue
   invent
   invest
   invite
   involve
   isn't
   issue
   itself
   jaundice
   justice
   keeping
   kidding
   kindle
   kingdom
   kitchen
   knowing
   lacking
   landing
   languish
   laughing
   leading
   learning
   leaving
   letting
   lighting

   limit
   linen
   liquid
   liquor
   listen
   little
   liver
   livid
   living
   looking
   losing
   lying
   magic
   making
   margin
   massive
   matching
   meaning
   meeting
   melting
   merit
   middle
   midnight
   midtown
   million
   minute
   mirror
   mischief
   missing
   mission
   mistake
   misty
   mixture
   morning
   motive
   moving

   mister/Mr.
   missus/Mrs.
   muffin
   music
   native
   nibble
   nothing
   notice
   office
   painting
   panic
   parking
   passing
   paving
   permit
   persist
   pickle
   picnic
   picture
   pigeon
   pillow
   pistol
   pitcher
   pittance
   pity
   placing
   planning
   plastic
   playing
   pointing
   portrait
   practice
   predict
   pressing
   pretty
   prison   ►

---

*This word has the letter *e* in a common word ending; the *e* is pronounced ɪ (see Appendix A).

ɪ IN TWO-SYLLABLE WORDS (*CONTINUED*)

◄

privy	service	striking
profit	serving	struggling
promise	setting	stupid
public	shaking	submit
publish	sharing	swimming
pulling	shining	tactic
putting	shopping	taking
quickly	showing	talking
racing	signal	teaching
raising	silly	telling
ranging	silver	testing
rapid	simple	therein
reaching	singing	thinking
reading	single	thinner
resist*	sister	tissue
riding	sitting	tonic
rigid	sixty	tourist
rigor	skipping	toxic
risen	slimming	trading
river	slipper	traffic
ruin	smiling	tragic
ruling	solid	training
running	something	tranquil
sailing	sorting	transmit
sampling	Spanish	tribute
sandwich	speaking	tricky
saving	spending	trigger
scissors	spirit	triple
searching	splendid	tripping
seeing	splinter	trying
seeking	staring	tunic
selfish	starting	turning
selling	sticky	unit
sending	stingy	until

►

---

*This word has the letter *e* in an unstressed first syllable; the *e* is pronounced ɪ (see Appendix A).

◄ using

using   waiting   window
valid   walking   winner
vicious   warning   winter
victim   washing   wisdom
vigor   watching   wishing
villa   wearing   within
villains   wedding   without
vision   wherein   women
visit   whisper   working
vivid   whistle   worship
voting   widow   written

ɪ IN WORDS OF THREE OR MORE SYLLABLES

ability   aspirin   clarity
arbitrator   assistant   classical
academic   Atlantic   classification
accident   atomic   clinical
accomplish   attitude   coincidence
activity   attractive   collective
addition   attribute   combination
administration   audition   commission
admission   authentic   commitment
aesthetic   authority   committee
Africa   authorization   commodity
agriculture   automatic   communication
alternative   availability   community
ambiguous   beautiful   comparison
ambition   benefit   competition
American   biological   complicate
amicable   capability   compliment
animal   capacity   composition
anniversary   capital   condition
anticipate   certify   confidence
antidote   characteristic   conservative
application   charity   consider
architecture   chemical   consistent
article   citizen   Constitution
artificial   civilization   contaminate
artistic   clarification   contingence   ►

I IN WORDS OF THREE OR MORE SYLLABLES (*CONTINUED*)

◄ continue	disaster	fellowship
contradict	discipline	festival
contribution	discontent	forbidden
conviction	discover	fortify
cooperative	discriminate	frivolous
counterfeit	discussion	fugitive
creative	disinfect	furniture
credible	disorganization	genuine
criminal	displacement	heroic
critical	disposal	hesitate
criticism	disposition	hidden
decision*	dispute	hideous
dedicate	distinction	historical
definition	distribution	history
definitive*	division	holiday
delicatessen	domestic	horrible
delicious*	dominant	hospital
deliver*	dramatic	hostility
democratic	dynamic	humanity
density	economic	humidifier
derision*	emphasis	identify
despicable*	episode	identity
destiny	epitaph	idiot
determination*	equipment*	ignorant
dictionary	ethical	illusion
difference	evidence	illustration
different	examine*	imagination
difficult	executive*	imitation
dignity	exhibit*	immature
dilemma	experiment*	immigrant
diligent	extraordinary*	immortal
dimension	facility	impatient
diplomatic	familiar	impeccable
direction	family	impediment
director	fantastic	impending
disappear	favorite	implication ►

*These words have the letter *e* in an unstressed first syllable; the *e* is pronounced
ɪ (see Appendix A).

◄   important

impossible

impression

incident

incisive

incredible

independent

indicate

indigestion

indirect

indispensable

individual

industry

inevitable

infection

infinite

inflammation

influence

information

ingredient

inherent

inhibit

initial

initiative

innocent

insertion

insolence

inspection

institution

instruction

instrument

insufficient

insurance

integration

intellectual

intelligence

intensity

intention

interference

interior

intermission

intermittent

internal

international

interpretation

interrupt

interval

intervention

interview

intimidate

introduce

invariably

invention

investigation

investment

invisible

irritate

jurisdiction

justify

leadership

legislation

liberty

limitation

linear

literally

literature

logical

magnetic

magnificent

majority

manipulate

mathematical

maturity

maximum

mechanical*

medicine

membership

metabolism*

metropolitan

military

milligram

minimal

minister

minority

miserable

mislead

monitor

morality

multiple

musical

narrative

negative

nutrition

obituary

objective

obligation

obliterate

oblivious

official

opinion

opportunity

opposite

optimum

ordinary

organic

organization

original

Pacific

participation

particular

peripheral   ►

---

*These words have the letter *e* in an unstressed first syllable; the *e* is pronounced
ɪ (see Appendix A).

I IN WORDS OF THREE OR MORE SYLLABLES (*CONTINUED*)

◄ permission
personality
perspective
pertinent
philosophy
pinnacle
pitiful
plausible
policy
politics
position
positive
possibility
practical
precision*
preliminary*
president
primarily
primitive
principle
prisoner
privilege
probability
productive
prognosis
prominent
prospective
provision
publication
publicity
purify
quality
quantity
radical

rapidly
realistic
reality
realization
recognition
refrigeration*
register
rehabilitation
relationship*
relative
religion*
representative
residence
residual*
responsibility*
ridiculous
ritual
romantic
sacrifice
satisfactory
scholarship
scientific
security*
seductive*
sensitive
significance
similar
situation
socialism
specialist
specific*
stabilization
statistic
stimulate

strategic
substitute
sufficient
superficial
supervision
suspicion
technical
television
temporarily
terrible
terrify
territory
testimony
theoretical
tradition
transition
trivial
uniform
unity
universal
university
utility
vanilla
vehicle
velocity*
victory
video
vigorous
violin
visible
visitor
visual
vitality
Washington

---

*These words have the letter *e* in an unstressed first syllable; the *e* is pronounced ɪ (see Appendix A).

ɪ WITH y SPELLING IN ONE-SYLLABLE WORDS

crypt	hymn	myth
cyst	lymph	nymph
gym	lynch	tryst

ɪ WITH y SPELLING IN TWO-SYLLABLE WORDS

Brooklyn	lyric	syndrome
cryptic	mystic	syntax
cymbal	physics	syringe
cynic	rhythm	syrup
crystal	symbol	system
gypsy	synapse	

ɪ WITH y SPELLING IN WORDS OF THREE OR MORE SYLLABLES

analysis	idiosyncrasy	symbolism
anonymous	myriad	sympathy
chrysanthemum	mystery	symphony
cylinder	Olympics	synagogue
dysfunction	oxygen	synchronize
glycerin	physical	syndicate
homonym	physician	synonym
hypnosis	pyramid	typical
hypocrisy	syllable	tyranny
hysterical	symbolic	

Note: The *-ing* suffix always uses the vowel ɪ.

Sentences: ɪ

CD
20

Turn to CD Track 20. Listen to the recording of the following sentences, then read the sentences aloud. Concentrate on correctly pronouncing the ɪ sound, which is marked phonetically.

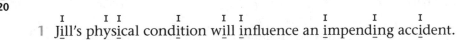

1 Jill's physical condition will influence an impending accident.

2 Bill introduced a combination of video images and still pictures.

3 It was a disaster when the drink spilled all over the clinical evidence.

4 The office had a policy of nondiscrimination for women.

5 She rapidly fingered the guitar strings, producing beautiful music.

6 The intern examined Mr. Miller's hip and indicated a positive prognosis.

7 The administration stressed the importance of interviews to the six

candidates.

8 In my opinion, physical activity is important.

9 I wish the script had been less typical and better written.

10 The menu consists mainly of squid and is quite limited.

11 I initially take aspirin when I practice my English.

12 Cindy's chronically bad vision caused her to make many mistakes

at the university.

13 Chris resisted building in a traditional and unimaginative architectural
style.

14 I imagine a plausible situation in which Bill's interests and intelligence

are utilized.

15 It is silly to begin dinner when Phil is still missing.

16 In the middle of the disaster, the thought of a tranquil dip in the Pacific

was calming.

17 The authorities sought the evidence to convict the convict in the

vicious assault.

18 We think Tim should reconsider the situation and admit to his guilt.

19 His inability to sit still compromised his willingness to finish the project.

20 My little sister is persistent in interfering in my business.

Sentences: ɪ vs. i

Turn to CD Track 21. Listen to the recording of the following sentences, then read the sentences aloud. Concentrate on distinguishing between the ɪ and i sounds, which are marked phonetically.

1 He insists his seemingly insignificant deed was a victory and

   an achievement.

2 Christie feels she's completely fulfilled her obligation in a meaningful way.

3 She dreams of having a sleek, discreet, and impeccably clean condo

   by the sea.

4 The insight of the team leader inspired the artistic productivity of all.

5 We agreed instantly that his team's mistakes created the disastrous

   conflict.

6 Lee needed clarification before proceeding, as the instructions were

   misleading.

7 Responsible people can complete a key project with impressive precision.

8 Sheila's metabolism increased with brisk walking and additional protein.

9 Keep believing that consistent practice leads to dramatic improvement.

10 His esteemed intelligence gives credibility to his unusual system

   of working.

11 Deep breathing increases circulation and improves vitality.

12 Is Tim satisfied with the quality of the steam machine?

13 Gina picked a tin of pickled beets to bring on the picnic.

14 Did you eat the beef sandwiches I was saving for dinner?

15 Teaching can frequently seem difficult, but it's rewarding.

16 The thief will keep stealing until he is apprehended.

17 Nick is quick-witted, genial, and completely motivated.

18 I definitely believe being determined and ambitious will lead to victory.

19 The festive city streets were appealing to Jean.

20 He seized the opportunity to interrupt the bizarre procedure.

For more details about the use of the vowel ɪ in prefixes and suffixes with unusual spelling patterns, see Appendix A.

TEN

The vowel e

The *e* sound defined

The short *e* sound, represented by the phonetic symbol e (as in *hem*), is a potential pronunciation problem for nonnative speakers of English. The *e* spelling pattern is used in other languages, but it is usually pronounced more openly, as ɛ, which is not used in English. The ɛ pronunciation is often substituted for the more closed e used by English. These two different vowel sounds are made very close to each other, but with a definite difference in tongue placement.

Like ɪ, which we discussed in the previous chapter, e is a front vowel: For both sounds, the tip of the tongue rests against the lower teeth and it is the arch in the front of the tongue that determines the phoneme. The difference in the arch is minuscule—about one-eighth of an inch between the two. The e vowel is usually spelled with *e*; it is also used in the suffix *-ary* (as in *secretary* and *ordinary*), as well as in the words *any* and *many*.

Step 1: Feeling the placement of *e*

DVD

8

*Turn now to **DVD Track 8**, where a step-by-step demonstration of the placement of e, in contrast to the placement of i and ɪ, is presented. After you have watched the DVD, read the following description of the sound placement and do the exercises below.

Take out your mirror. Begin by saying the i sound. Say the word *he* several times. Looking in the mirror, check the placement of your tongue. Notice that the tip of your tongue is resting against your lower teeth and that the front of your tongue is arched forward. You can check yourself by placing the tip of your little finger on the top edge of your lower teeth, as demonstrated on the DVD exercise. Feel the arch in the front of your tongue as it contacts your finger when you say *he*.

Drop the arch in the front of your tongue back about one-eighth of an inch, leaving the tip of your tongue against your lower teeth. This is the placement of the vowel ɪ, as described in the previous chapter. Say i . . . *he* . . . ɪ . . . *him*.

Now, drop the arch in the front of your tongue back about an additional one-eighth of an inch. This is e . . . *hem*. Say these three front vowels as you feel the arch in the front of your tongue drop back about one-eighth of an inch for the next phoneme: i . . . ɪ . . . e . . . *he* . . . *him* . . . *hem*.

Return now to **DVD Track 8**. Practice the difference in placement among the vowels i, ɪ, and e.

Step 2: Hearing the placement of *e*

Using the mirror, look closely inside your mouth. Move your tongue back and forth between the placements of these three words: *he, him, hem* . . . *he, him, hem* . . . *he, him, hem*. (Of course, your lips will come together for the consonant m.)

Watch in the mirror as you pronounce the pairs of words in the following list. Listen to the differences between ɛ and e, so that you can train your ear to hear the distinction, as well as feel the physiological difference in placement.

Note: In previous chapters (except Chapter Five), the sound placement for each new phoneme was contrasted with that of another, frequently substituted phoneme. However, since no words in English use ɛ, the words in the list are the same in both columns. The purpose of the exercise is to pronounce each word incorrectly with ɛ, then correctly with e. The difference between the two is recorded on the accompanying CD.

ɛ (INCORRECT)	e (CORRECT)
b<u>e</u>t	b<u>e</u>t
c<u>e</u>nt	c<u>e</u>nt
fr<u>e</u>sh	fr<u>e</u>sh
g<u>e</u>t	g<u>e</u>t
m<u>e</u>lt	m<u>e</u>lt
n<u>e</u>xt	n<u>e</u>xt
pl<u>e</u>dge	pl<u>e</u>dge
th<u>e</u>n	th<u>e</u>n
r<u>e</u>nt	r<u>e</u>nt
f<u>e</u>ll	f<u>e</u>ll
th<u>e</u>m	th<u>e</u>m
m<u>a</u>ny	m<u>a</u>ny
fr<u>e</u>t	fr<u>e</u>t
wh<u>e</u>n	wh<u>e</u>n
y<u>e</u>s	y<u>e</u>s

CD
22

Turn now to CD Track 22, which features the sound adjustments between ɛ and e. Repeat the pairs of words, while comparing your pronunciation with that on the CD.

Record your own pronunciation, and compare it to the CD track. Repeat this exercise until you feel ready to proceed to the next step.

Step 3: Applying the placement of *e*

Following are lists of common English words that contain the e sound. You can practice this sound by reading these lists aloud. After you have mastered the sound, advance to the sentences in the next section.

e IN ONE-SYLLABLE WORDS

b<u>e</u>d	b<u>e</u>lt	b<u>e</u>st
b<u>e</u>g	b<u>e</u>nch	b<u>e</u>t
b<u>e</u>ll	b<u>e</u>nt	bl<u>e</u>nd ▶

e IN ONE-SYLLABLE WORDS (*CONTINUED*)

◄

bless	fresh	realm
bread	fret	red
breast	friend	rent
breath	get	rep
bred	guess	rest
cell	guest	said
cent	head	self
check	health	sell
chef	held	send
chess	hell	sense
chest	help	shed
clench	hem	shelf
crept	hen	shell
crest	jet	shred
dead	kept	sketch
deaf	led	sled
debt*	left	smell
deck	lend	sped
delve	lens	spell
den	less	spend
dense	meant	stem
dent	melt	step
depth	men	strength
desk	met	stress
dread	neck	stretch
dress	nest	swell
dwell	next	tempt
edge	peg	ten
else	pen	tend
end	pest	tent
fed	pet	test
fell	pledge	text
fence	press	them
fled	quench	then
flesh	quest	thread

►

---

*The *b* in this word is silent and not pronounced.

◄
thr<u>ea</u>t	w<u>e</u>b	wh<u>e</u>n
tr<u>ea</u>d	w<u>e</u>ll	wr<u>e</u>ck
tr<u>e</u>nd	w<u>e</u>nt	wr<u>e</u>nch
v<u>e</u>nt	w<u>e</u>pt	y<u>e</u>s
v<u>e</u>st	w<u>e</u>st	y<u>e</u>t
v<u>e</u>t	w<u>e</u>t	z<u>e</u>st

Certain spelling patterns with *e* in a prefix or suffix are pronounced as ɪ, and therefore not underlined in the next two lists. See Appendix A for details.

e IN TWO-SYLLABLE WORDS

-<u>a</u>ry (*suffix*)	c<u>e</u>ntral	def<u>e</u>ct
acc<u>e</u>nt	ch<u>e</u>mist	def<u>e</u>nd
acc<u>e</u>pt	ch<u>e</u>rish	defl<u>e</u>ct
addr<u>e</u>ss	ch<u>e</u>rry	dej<u>e</u>ct
ad<u>e</u>pt	cl<u>e</u>ver	d<u>e</u>ntist
ag<u>ai</u>n	coll<u>e</u>ct	dep<u>e</u>nd
ag<u>ai</u>nst	comm<u>e</u>nce	det<u>e</u>ct
am<u>e</u>nd	comm<u>e</u>nd	det<u>e</u>st
<u>a</u>ny	comm<u>e</u>nt	d<u>e</u>vil
asc<u>e</u>nd	comp<u>e</u>l	dig<u>e</u>st
asp<u>e</u>ct	compl<u>e</u>x	div<u>e</u>st
ass<u>e</u>ss	compr<u>e</u>ss	<u>e</u>cho
ass<u>e</u>ts	conc<u>e</u>pt	<u>e</u>dit
att<u>e</u>mpt	cond<u>e</u>nse	eff<u>e</u>ct
att<u>e</u>nd	conf<u>e</u>ss	<u>e</u>ffort
att<u>e</u>st	cong<u>e</u>st	el<u>e</u>ct
av<u>e</u>nge	conn<u>e</u>ct	<u>e</u>mpty
b<u>e</u>lly	cont<u>e</u>mpt	<u>e</u>ngine
b<u>e</u>rry	cont<u>e</u>nt	<u>e</u>nter
b<u>e</u>tter	cont<u>e</u>st	<u>e</u>ntrance
bis<u>e</u>ct	cont<u>e</u>xt	<u>e</u>nvy
br<u>ea</u>kfast	conv<u>e</u>nt	<u>e</u>rrand
b<u>u</u>ry	cr<u>e</u>dit	<u>e</u>rror
cad<u>e</u>t	cr<u>e</u>scent	<u>e</u>ssay
cem<u>e</u>nt	cr<u>e</u>vice	<u>e</u>thics
c<u>e</u>nsure	d<u>e</u>bit	<u>e</u>thnic
c<u>e</u>nter	d<u>e</u>cade	ev<u>e</u>nt

►

e IN TWO-SYLLABLE WORDS (*CONTINUED*)

◄

ever	lemon	rebel (*noun*)
excerpt	length	record (*noun*)
exhale	letter	reflect
expect	level	reflex
expend	many	regret
expense	measure	repress
expert	member	rescue
express	mental	respect
extend	mention	revenge
extra	menu	second
feather	merit	section
ferry	message	segment
forget	metal	seldom
freckle	method	select
frenzy	neglect	sentence
gender	nephew	separate
gentle	never	session
gesture	pebble	seven
heaven	peddle	shelter
heavy	penny	shepherd
hectic	pension	sheriff
helmet	pepper	skeptic
immense	peril	special
impend	perish	spectrum
impress	pleasure	success
indent	plenty	suggest
index	precious	suppress
inept	preface	suspect
inflect	premise	suspend
intend	present (*noun, adjective*)	temper
intense	pressure	tempo
invest	pretend	tender
jealous	prevent	tennis
kettle	project	tenor
leather	protest	tension
lecture	question	terrace
legend	ready	terror

►

◄
treasure	vendor	welcome
tremble	venue	welfare
trespass	very	whether
unless	vessel	wrestle
upset	weather	yellow
velvet	wedding	zealous

e IN WORDS OF THREE OR MORE SYLLABLES

accelerate	cemetery	dialect
accessible	century	dictionary
accessory	cessation	dilemma
addendum	clientele	dimension
adventure	comprehend	direction
aesthetic	conception	discrepancy
affection	condescend	disinfect
agenda	confection	dispensable
aggression	conjecture	disseminate
America	consecutive	domestic
ancestor	consequence	eccentric
anesthetize	contemporary	edible
antiseptic	correction	educate
apathetic	credible	election
appendix	crescendo	electric
apprehend	deception	elegant
apprehension	decorate	element
architect	dedicate	elephant
assemble	deficit	elevate
attention	definite	eleven
benefit	delicate	embezzle
beverage	demonstrate	emerald
burial	deposition	empathy
calisthenics	deprecate	emulate
celebrate	designate	enemy
celebrity	desperate	energy
celery	destiny	entity
celestial	devastate	equity
cellophane	develop	especially

►

e IN WORDS OF THREE OR MORE SYLLABLES (*CONTINUED*)

◄

essential	memory	reprehensible
estimate	mesmerize	reputation
everything	metaphor	retrospect
evidence	necessary	revenue
evolution	negative	reverence
excellent	objective	secretary
excessive	pedigree	sedentary
execute	penalty	seminar
exercise	percentage	sentiment
experiment	phonetic	separate
extrovert	predicate	September
February	prejudice	serendipity
feminine	preparation	severance
festival	presentation	specify
fiduciary	president	speculate
flexible	pretentious	subjective
general	profession	supremacy
generation	progression	surrender
generous	propensity	susceptible
genuine	reception	telephone
heritage	recession	television
hesitate	recipe	temperature
identity	recognition	temporary
impeccable	recommend	territory
incentive	reconcile	testify
infection	rectify	therapy
inherit	reference	together
intelligent	reflexive	umbrella
jeopardize	register	utensil
legacy	regular	vegetable
legislation	remember	verify
medical	renovate	yesterday
melody	repetition	

Sentences: *e*

*Turn to **CD Track 23***. Listen to the recording of the following sentences, then read the sentences aloud. Concentrate on correctly pronouncing the e sound, which is marked phonetically.

       e   e   e   e   e   e
1 In retrospect, I recognize the merits of the intense seminar.

      e   e   e   e   e   e
2 Against better judgment, Erin commenced the event with a lecture

     e
on health.

      e   e   e   e   e
3 When under stress, you should stretch, rest, and exercise.

       e   e   e   e   e   e
4 Did Ken's letter mention that he spent Wednesday with my best

     e
friend?

      e   e   e   e
5 The expert expressed an immense desire to win the contest.

        e   e   e   e   e
6 Are you compelled to attend a session on the trends of bank lending?

      e   e   e   e   e
7 When can Jerry collect his well-earned pension?

      e   e   e   e
8 In the hectic frenzy, the more minor errands were neglected.

       e   e   e   e   e
9 The protesters outside the tent were met with threatening gestures.

    e   e   e   e   e   e
10 Members of the press speculated about the presidential election.

       e   e   e   e   e   e
11 Did you ever expect the heavy pressure to divest your assets?

   e   e   e   e   e   e
12 I guessed that Ted fretted and vented when faced with an error.

   e   e   e   e   e   e
13 Ethically, can Evan try to get a "yes" from every guest?

      e   e   e   e
14 Did you intend for your clever comment to be taken out of context?

   e   e   e   e
15 Measure the ingredients before attempting any estimate to a recipe.

16 He recommended ending a devastating debt through temporary but select credit.

17 Discrepancy in the project's professional preparation could have jeopardizing effects.

18 I suggest avoiding regrets when delving into the past.

19 The melody was mesmerizing, especially as it accelerated toward the crescendo.

20 The chef's impeccable presentation kept the menu fresh and the clientele dedicated.

ELEVEN

The vowel æ

The æ sound defined

The short *a* sound, represented by the phonetic symbol æ (as in *ham*), is often mispronounced by nonnative speakers of English. Depending on a person's native language, the vowel æ can be pronounced too tightly, like ɛ, or too openly, like ɑ.

Like e, which was discussed in the previous chapter, æ is a front vowel: For both sounds, the tip of the tongue rests against the lower teeth and it is the arch in the front of the tongue that determines the phoneme. The difference in the arch is minuscule—about one-eighth of an inch between the two. The æ vowel is always spelled with *a*.

Step 1: Feeling the placement of æ

*Turn now to **DVD Track 9**,* where a step-by-step demonstration of the placement of æ, in contrast to the placement of i, ɪ, and e, is presented. After you have watched the DVD, read the following description of the sound placement and do the exercises below.

Take out your mirror. Begin by saying the i sound. Then say the word *he* several times. Looking in the mirror, check the placement of your tongue. Notice that the tip of your tongue is resting against your lower teeth and that the front of your tongue is arched forward. You can check

117

yourself by placing the tip of your little finger on the top edge of your lower teeth, as demonstrated on the DVD exercise. Feel the arch in the front of your tongue as it contacts your finger when you say *he*.

Drop the arch in the front of your tongue back about one-eighth of an inch, leaving the tip of your tongue against your lower teeth. This is the placement of the vowel ɪ. Now, drop the arch in the front of your tongue back about an additional one-eighth of an inch, as described in the previous chapter. This is e. Say these first three front vowels as you feel the arch in the front of your tongue drop back about one-eighth of an inch for the next phoneme: i . . . ɪ . . . e . . . *he . . . him . . . hem*.

Now, drop the arch in the front of your tongue back about an additional one-eighth of an inch. This is æ . . . *ham*. Say all four front vowels as you feel the arch in the front of your tongue drop back about one-eighth of an inch for the next phoneme: i . . . ɪ . . . e . . . æ . . . *he . . . him . . . hem . . . ham*.

Now that you've located the placement of æ, let's contrast æ with ɑ. As demonstrated on the DVD, put your little finger back in your mouth and say æ. Then, drop your tongue flat onto the floor of your mouth. This is ɑ. Go back and forth between the two placements: æ . . . ɑ . . . æ . . . ɑ . . . æ . . . ɑ.

*Return now to **DVD Track 9**.* Practice the difference in placement among the vowels i, ɪ, e, and æ, as well as the physical contrast between æ and ɑ.

Step 2: Hearing the placement of æ

Using the mirror, look closely inside your mouth. Move your tongue back and forth between the placements of these four words: *he, him, hem, ham . . . he, him, hem, ham . . . he, him, hem, ham*. (Of course, your lips will come together for the consonant m.)

Watch in the mirror as you pronounce the pairs of words in the following list. Listen to the vowel sound changes, so that you can train your ear to hear the distinction, as well as feel the physiological difference in placement.

e	æ
b<u>e</u>t	b<u>a</u>t
b<u>e</u>g	b<u>a</u>g
s<u>e</u>t	s<u>a</u>t
fl<u>e</u>sh	fl<u>a</u>sh
gu<u>e</u>ss	g<u>a</u>s
n<u>e</u>ck	kn<u>a</u>ck*
m<u>e</u>ss	m<u>a</u>ss
p<u>e</u>n	p<u>a</u>n
t<u>e</u>n	t<u>a</u>n
wr<u>e</u>ck*	r<u>a</u>ck
l<u>e</u>nd	l<u>a</u>nd
m<u>e</u>n	m<u>a</u>n
s<u>e</u>nd	s<u>a</u>nd
b<u>e</u>nd	b<u>a</u>nd
v<u>e</u>t	v<u>a</u>t

CD

24

*Turn now to **CD Track 24**,* which features the sound adjustments between e and æ. Repeat the pairs of words, while comparing your pronunciation with that on the CD.

Record your own pronunciation, and compare it to the CD track. Repeat this exercise until you feel ready to proceed to the next step.

Step 3: Applying the placement of æ

Following are lists of common English words that contain the æ sound. In addition, there is an "answer" list, which contains common words where an *a* spelling is pronounced with ɑ in British English, but with æ in American English. You can practice the æ sound by reading these lists aloud. After you have mastered the sound, advance to the sentences in the next section.

---

*When the *kn* or *wr* spelling pattern occurs at the beginning of a syllable or word, the *k* or *w* is silent and not pronounced.

æ IN ONE-SYLLABLE WORDS

act	clang	jazz
add	clap	knack
and	clash	lab
ash	crab	lack
at	crack	lag
ax	cramp	lamb
back	crank	lamp
bad	crash	land
badge	crass	lapse
bag	dad	lash
ban	damp	mad
band	dash	man
bang	drab	map
bank	drag	mass
bash	fact	mat
bat	fan	match
batch	fax	math
blab	flag	nag
black	flap	nap
bland	flash	pack
blank	flat	pact
brag	frank	pad
bran	gag	pal
brand	gang	pan
brat	gap	pants
cab	gas	patch
camp	glad	plaid
can	grab	plan
cap	grand	prank
cash	hack	rack
cat	ham	rag
catch	hand	ran
chap	hang	ranch
chat	hat	rang
clad	hatch	rank
clam	hath	rash
clamp	have	rat
clan	jam	sack

►

◄ s<u>a</u>d

s<u>a</u>g

s<u>a</u>nd

s<u>a</u>ng

s<u>a</u>t

sc<u>a</u>lp

scr<u>a</u>p

scr<u>a</u>tch

sh<u>a</u>ck

sh<u>a</u>ll

sl<u>a</u>b

sl<u>a</u>ck

sl<u>a</u>m

sl<u>a</u>ng

sl<u>a</u>p

sm<u>a</u>sh

sn<u>a</u>ck

sn<u>a</u>g

sn<u>a</u>p

sp<u>a</u>n

sp<u>a</u>sm

st<u>a</u>b

st<u>a</u>ck

st<u>a</u>ff

st<u>a</u>mp

st<u>a</u>nd

str<u>a</u>nd

str<u>a</u>p

t<u>a</u>ck

t<u>a</u>g

t<u>a</u>n

t<u>a</u>p

t<u>a</u>sk

t<u>a</u>x

th<u>a</u>nk

th<u>a</u>t

tr<u>a</u>ck

tr<u>a</u>mp

tr<u>a</u>nce

tr<u>a</u>p

tr<u>a</u>sh

v<u>a</u>lve

v<u>a</u>n

v<u>a</u>t

w<u>a</u>g

w<u>a</u>x

wr<u>a</u>p

wr<u>a</u>th

y<u>a</u>nk

æ IN TWO-SYLLABLE WORDS

<u>a</u>bbey

<u>a</u>bsent

<u>a</u>bstr<u>a</u>ct

<u>a</u>ccent

<u>a</u>cid

<u>a</u>ctive

<u>a</u>ctress

ad<u>a</u>pt

<u>a</u>ddict (*noun*)

<u>a</u>dverb

<u>a</u>gile

al<u>a</u>s

<u>a</u>lbum

<u>a</u>lley

<u>a</u>loe

<u>a</u>mber

<u>a</u>mbush

<u>a</u>mple

<u>a</u>nchor

<u>a</u>ngle

<u>a</u>ngry

<u>a</u>nguish

<u>a</u>nkle

<u>a</u>nnex

<u>a</u>nti

<u>a</u>ntique

<u>a</u>ntler

<u>a</u>nxious

<u>a</u>pple

<u>a</u>rid

<u>a</u>rrow

<u>a</u>shes

<u>a</u>sset

<u>a</u>sthma

<u>a</u>stral

<u>a</u>tlas

<u>a</u>tom

att<u>a</u>ched

att<u>a</u>ck

<u>a</u>ttic

attr<u>a</u>ct

<u>a</u>vid

b<u>a</u>ffle

b<u>a</u>lance

b<u>a</u>llet

b<u>a</u>llot

b<u>a</u>ndit

b<u>a</u>nish

b<u>a</u>nner

b<u>a</u>nquet

b<u>a</u>nter

b<u>a</u>rrel

b<u>a</u>rren

b<u>a</u>ttle

beg<u>a</u>n

bl<u>a</u>dder

bl<u>a</u>nket

►

æ IN TWO-SYLLABLE WORDS (*CONTINUED*)

◄ bracket   compact   haddock
brandy   contact   hadn't
cabbage   contract   hammer
cactus   cracker   hamper
caffeine   dagger   handle
camel   damage   happen
campus   dandruff   happy
canal   dangle   hasn't
cancel   dazzle   haven't
candid   detach   havoc
candle   detract   hazard
candor   dispatch   impact
candy   distract   intact
canon   drastic   jacket
canteen   exact   jagged
canyon   exam   lackey
capsule   expand   ladder
captain   fabric   language
caption   facile   Latin
captive   factor   latter
carrot   fancy   madam
carry   fashion   magic
cascade   finance   malice
cashew   flashlight   manage
cashmere   flatter   manic
catcher   fraction   mansion
cattle   fragile   married
cavern   fragment   matter
challenge   frantic   narrow
champagne   gadget   package
channel   gallon   packet
chapel   gamble   pamper
chapter   garish   panel
chatter   gather   panic
clamor   glamour   passion
clatter   grammar   passive
climax   grapple   pattern
collapse   habit   perhaps ►

◄ phantom
planet
plastic
practice
protract
rabbit
racket
ramble
rampant
random
rapid
rattle
relax
romance
salad
salmon
salvage
sample
sanction
sandwich
satire
scaffold
scandal

scramble
shadow
shampoo
slander
Spanish
sparrow
spasm
stagger
stagnant
standard
static
statue
status
stature
strangle
subtract
tackle
tactic
talent
tamper
tango
tatter
traffic

tranquil
transcend
transcribe
transcript
transfer
transform
transfused
transit
translate
transmit
transpire
transverse
travel
vaccine
vacuum
valid
valiant
valley
vanish
vapid
wagon

æ IN WORDS OF THREE OR MORE SYLLABLES

abandon
abdicate
abdomen
abnormal
absolute
abstinence
academy
accident
accurate
accusation
acquisition
acrobat
actual

adamant
adequate
adjective
admirable
admiral
adolescence
adoration
adversary
advertise
advocate
affable
affidavit
affirmation

affluent
Africa
aggravate
agitate
agony
agriculture
alcohol
alfalfa
algebra
alibi
alkaline
allegation
allergy ►

æ IN WORDS OF THREE OR MORE SYLLABLES (*CONTINUED*)

◀

alligator	asterisk	catholic
allocate	astronaut	cavalcade
alphabet	atmosphere	cavalry
altitude	atrophy	cavity
altruism	attitude	ceramic
alveolar	attribute (*noun*)	champion
amalgam	avarice	chandelier
amateur	avenue	character
ambassador	average	chariot
ambiguous	bachelor	charitable
ambulance	bacteria	charity
amicable	balcony	circumstance
amnesty	banana	clarify
amorous	bandana	collaborate
amplify	baptism	companion
amputate	barricade	comparison
anagram	brutality	congratulate
analogy	cabaret	contaminate
analysis	cafeteria	dialysis
ancestor	calcium	diameter
anecdote	calculate	diaphragm
animal	calendar	diplomat
animate	caliber	distraction
anniversary	calisthenics	dramatic
annual	calorie	dynamic
antagonism	camouflage	elaborate
anticipate	candidate	elastic
antidote	canopy	embarrass
antiseptic	cantaloupe	erratic
anxiety	capital	evacuate
apparent	caravan	evaluation
appetite	casserole	evaporate
application	castigate	exacerbate
apprehend	casually	exact
aptitude	catalyst	exaggerate
arrogance	catastrophe	examine
aspirate	category	exasperate
aspirin	caterpillar	extraction

▶

◄ extravagant
fabulous
faculty
family
fantastic
fascination
financial
galaxy
gallery
gasoline
gigantic
gradually
graduate
gratitude
gravity
guarantee
handicap
hospitality
humanity
imagine
infallible
international
January
laboratory
laminate
lateral
magazine

magnify
majesty
management
manager
mandatory
manifest
mannequin
manual
manufacture
masculine
masterpiece
matrimony
morality
mortality
national
natural
palatable
palpable
palpitate
paradise
parallel
parody
piano
practical
pragmatic
ramification
ratify

rationalize
reaction
retraction
sacrifice
sanctity
sanitary
sanity
satisfaction
Saturday
spectacular
stamina
strategy
substantial
tangible
tantalize
tragedy
transaction
transcription
transition
transportation
understand
vacillate
valuable
vernacular
vitality
vocabulary

THE "ANSWER" LIST: æ IN ONE-SYLLABLE WORDS

ask	brass	chance
bask	calf*	chant
bath	calve*	clasp
blanch	can't	class
blast	cask	craft
branch	cast	dance ►

---

*When the *alf* or *alv* spelling pattern occurs at the end of a syllable or word, the *l* is silent and not pronounced.

THE "ANSWER" LIST: æ IN ONE-SYLLABLE WORDS (CONTINUED)

◄

draft	half*	raft
fast	halve*	rasp
flask	lance	shaft
France	last	slant
gasp	laugh	staff
glance	mask	task
glass	mast	trance
graft	pass	vast
grant	past	waft
graph	path	wrath
grasp	plant	
grass	prance	

THE "ANSWER" LIST: æ IN TWO-SYLLABLE WORDS

advance	enchant	pasture
after	enhance	plaster
alas	fasten	rascal
answer	forecast	rather
basket	ghastly	sample
behalf	giraffe	slander
casket	lather	transplant†
castle	master	trespass
command	nasty	vantage
demand	pastor	

THE "ANSWER" LIST: æ IN WORDS OF THREE OR MORE SYLLABLES

advantage†	disaster	raspberry
avalanche†	example	reprimand
chancellor	flabbergast†	telegraph
disadvantage	paragraph†	

---

*When the *alf* or *alv* spelling pattern occurs at the end of a syllable or word, the *l* is silent and not pronounced.

†In these words, both *a* spellings are pronounced æ in American English. In British English, the first *a* is pronounced æ and the second is pronounced ɑ.

Sentences: æ

*Turn to **CD Track 25**.* Listen to the recording of the following sentences, then read the sentences aloud. Concentrate on correctly pronouncing the æ sound, which is marked phonetically.

1 Mandy is a talented actress who admires the impact of transformative theater.

2 Looking back, Max was glad he had not made a pact and signed a contract.

3 Before the banquet, we served crackers, cheese, clams, and champagne.

4 Sandy managed to translate the classic transcript into four languages.

5 He's planning on transferring a substantial number of credits for his bachelor's degree.

6 Rather than advocating collaboration, the candidates seemed ambiguous.

7 It takes stamina to manifest desires into tangible matter.

8 Frankly, I prefer answering my phone to texting; I like human contact.

9 Are you satisfied with your manager's pragmatic evaluation process?

10 Chad added tango melodies to his jazz band's practice.

Sentences: æ vs. e

*Turn to **CD Track 26**.* Listen to the recording of the following sentences, then read the sentences aloud. Concentrate on distinguishing between the æ and e sounds, which are marked phonetically.

      e   æ   e   e   e   æ e   e æ   æ

1 Fred was apprehensive when addressing his accent, yet tackled practice

         æ

with vitality.

  æ   æ   æ   æ   æ   e

2 Advancing in status within the bank's branch depended on

     e   e

demonstrating credibility.

       æ   e   e   e

3 Some answers will present themselves through quieting excessive

   e   æ

mental chatter.

    æ   æ   e   e   æ

4 The advocate abandoned his reflexively pretentious mask.

    æ   æ   e   e   æ   æ

5 The accident aggravated Ben's intense abdominal cramps.

  æ   æ   æ æ   e   æ   e

6 Acting crassly and arrogantly seldom commands respect.

      e   æ e   æ   æ   æ æ

7 What serendipity to transcend both grandstanding and actively

    æ   e

slandering reputations!

       e   æ   æ æ   æ æ

8 The weather forecaster predicted damp afternoons and patchy fog

    æ   e e

patterns in February.

       æ   e   æ   æ   e   e

9 The plan to disseminate Anne's financial records was unpleasant

      e e

but necessary.

     æ   e æ   e æ   e

10 Does altitude affect attitude when traveling domestically?

     e   æ   e   æ   æ   æ

11 The tennis match between Eric and Matthew was challenging.

    æ   e   æ æ   e   æ

12 Caffeine is a mood elevator, but can have the negative impact of

       æ

causing anxiety.

13 Can you comprehend the baffling concept, or is it too protracted

and inaccessible?

14 Andrew's apparent sense of supremacy made him appear arrogant

and condescending.

15 Maggie worked absolute magic in the editing room, yet everything

seemed effortless.

Sentences: æ vs. ɑ

*Turn to **CD Track 27**.* Listen to the recording of the following sentences, then read the sentences aloud. Concentrate on distinguishing between the æ and ɑ sounds, which are marked phonetically.

1 Jan was happily distracted by watching espionage films.

2 The anniversary celebration happened on a balmy afternoon

in Washington.

3 Dashing Angelo was a suave renaissance man with both bravado

and laughter.

4 The romantic aria was enchanting and created an amorous atmosphere.

5 Can accurate and specific information be camouflaged in nuance?

6 After cranking out the massive project, I deserved a calming massage.

7 Would you prefer a pasta casserole, or a salad with avocado and alfalfa
sprouts?

8 For a finale, the soprano sang Rodgers and Hammerstein's "Shall We
   Dance?"
   (ɑ: finale; ɑ: soprano; æ: sang; ɑ: Rodgers; æ: Hammerstein; æ: Shall; æ: Dance)

9 Examples of English alphabet spelling can't accurately explain the
   schwa phoneme.
   (æ: Examples; æ: alphabet; æ: can't; æ: accurately; ɑ: schwa)

10 Adding palm trees to the façade of the spa enhanced the relaxing
   ambience.
   (æ: Adding; ɑ: palm; ɑ: façade; ɑ: spa; æ: enhanced; æ: relaxing; ɑ: ambience; ɑ: ambience)

11 They called "Bravo!" after the amateur cabaret's climax.
   (ɑ: Bravo; æ: after; æ: amateur; æ: cabaret's; æ: climax)

12 Unimaginable circumstances made Father feel swamped and agitated
   by his calendar.
   (æ: Unimaginable; æ: circumstances; ɑ: Father; ɑ: swamped; æ: and; æ: agitated; æ: calendar)

13 Macho police squad dramas are depicted on national television.
   (ɑ: Macho; ɑ: squad; ɑ: dramas; ɑ: on; æ: national)

14 Brad qualified to compete in the black belt karate match.
   (æ: Brad; ɑ: qualified; æ: black; ɑ: karate; æ: match)

15 Which would you rather magnify—a product's quantity or its quality?
   (æ: rather; æ: magnify; ɑ: product's; ɑ: quantity; ɑ: quality)

TWELVE

The vowels of r (ɝ and ɚ)

The ɝ/ɚ sounds defined

The vowels of *r*, represented by the phonetic symbols ɝ (in a stressed syllable) and ɚ (in an unstressed syllable) are frequently mispronounced by nonnative speakers of English. Depending on your native language, you may pronounce the vowels of *r* too tightly, because of too much tension in the back of your tongue. Or the *r* coloring may be dropped, because the tip of your tongue is touching your lower teeth.

Step 1: Feeling the placement of ɝ/ɚ

*Turn now to **DVD Track 10**,* where a step-by-step demonstration of the placement of the vowels ɝ/ɚ is presented. After you have watched the DVD, read the following description of the sound placement and do the exercises below.

DVD
10

These two *r* vowels are sounded the same; they have different phonetic representations because of the syllable stress within words (see Chapter Seventeen for a detailed explanation of syllable stress). Stressed syllables within words are enunciated with more emphasis and are typically longer, louder, and higher in pitch than unstressed syllables. The vowel ɝ is used in a stressed syllable within a word. The unstressed vowel ɚ marks a syllable as shorter and lower in pitch.

Take out your mirror. Let's examine the position of the tongue in forming the vowels ɝ/ɚ. Begin by placing the tip of your tongue against

131

your lower teeth, with your tongue lying flat on the floor of your mouth. Now, lift only the tip of your tongue and say ɝ.

To produce the consonant *r*, the sides of your tongue touch the inside of your upper teeth and your tongue is lifted close to the alveolar ridge. By contrast, to pronounce the vowels of *r*, ɝ/ɚ, the tip of your tongue is lifted only slightly, no higher than the bottom of your upper teeth, and the sides of your tongue do not make contact anywhere inside your mouth.

The most difficult problem you will have with the ɝ/ɚ placement is a tendency toward tongue retraction. Because the tip of your tongue isn't touching anywhere inside your mouth, the back of your tongue may tense and pull backward to feel "anchored." As demonstrated on the DVD, place your thumb under your jaw at the base of your tongue. Hold your thumb there firmly as you lift only the tip of your tongue. This will prevent your tongue from retracting backward.

Return now to **DVD Track 10.** Practice the placement of the vowels ɝ/ɚ.

Step 2: Hearing the placement of ɝ/ɚ

Using the mirror, look closely inside your mouth. Say ɝ . . . ɚ . . . ɝ . . . ɚ. Hear that the two vowels sound the same, except that ɝ has more emphasis and is longer and higher in pitch than ɚ. The examples of the words *hurt* (ɝ) and *other* (ɚ) demonstrate this. The tip of your tongue is lifted only slightly for both, no higher than the bottom of your upper teeth, and the sides of your tongue should not be touching anywhere inside your mouth.

Watch in the mirror as you pronounce the pairs of words in the following list. Listen to the vowel sound changes, so that you can train your ear to hear the distinction, as well as feel the physiological placement.

ɝ	ɚ
m<u>er</u>ger	merg<u>er</u>
mu<u>r</u>der	murd<u>er</u>
mu<u>r</u>mur	murm<u>ur</u>
nu<u>r</u>ture	nurt<u>ur</u>e ►

ɝ	ɚ
purpose	paper
adverse	adversary
affirm	affirmation
circle	circulation
confer	conference
observe	observation
perfume (*noun*)	perfume (*verb*)
prefer	preference
survey (*noun*)	survey (*verb*)

CD
28

Turn now to **CD Track 28**, which features the pronunciation of ɝ and ɚ. Repeat the pairs of words, while comparing your pronunciation with that on the CD.

Record your own pronunciation, and compare it to the CD track. Repeat this exercise until you feel ready to proceed to the next step.

Note: The first four sets of words contain both the strong ɝ and ɚ vowels and are read only once on the CD.

Step 3: Applying the placement of ɝ/ɚ

Following are lists of common English words that contain the ɝ and ɚ sounds. You can practice this sound by reading these lists aloud. After you have mastered the sound, advance to the sentences in the next section.

ɝ IN ONE-SYLLABLE WORDS

birch	churn	earn
bird	clerk	earth
birth	curb	err
blur	curl	firm
blurb	curse	first
blurt	curt	flirt
burn	curve	fur
burst	dirge	girl
chirp	dirt	girth

ɝ IN ONE-SYLLABLE WORDS (CONTINUED)

◄

heard	search	turn
her	serve	urge
herb*	shirt	urn
herd	sir	verb
hurl	skirt	verge
hurt	smirk	verse
irk	splurge	were
jerk	spur	weren't
learn	spurn	whirl
lurk	spurt	word
mirth	stern	work
nurse	stir	world
pearl	surf	worm
per	surge	worse
perch	term	worst
perk	terse	worth
pert	third	yearn
purr	thirst	
purse	turf	

ɝ IN TWO-SYLLABLE WORDS

absurd	circus	curry
accursed	clergy	curtain
adjourn	coerce	curtsy
adverse	colonel†	desert (verb)
affirm	concern	deserve
alert	concur	dessert
assert	confer	deter
averse	confirm	discern
avert	converge	disperse
burlap	converse	disturb
certain	convert	diverge
circle	curfew	diverse
circuit	current	divert

►

---

*The *h* in *herb* is silent and not pronounced in American English.

†*Colonel* is the only English word that contains an r pronunciation but has no *r*.

◄ early
earnest
emerge
ergo
exert
fertile
fervor
flourish
furbish
furnace
furnish
further
furtive
gurgle
hermit
hurdle
hurry
immerse
infer
infirm
insert (*verb*)
journal
journey

merchant
mercy
merger
murder
murky
murmur
nurture
observe
occur
overt
perfect (*adjective*)
perfume (*noun*)
person
perturbed
prefer
purchase
purple
purpose
recur
refer
research (*verb*)
reserve
return

serpent
sturdy
submerge
superb
surcharge
surface
surgeon
surplus
survey (*noun*)
thirty
thorough
Thursday
transfer (*verb*)
turkey
turmoil
turnip
turquoise
turtle
urban
usurp
worry
worship

ɝ IN WORDS OF THREE OR MORE SYLLABLES

allergic
alternative
anniversary
aspersion
attorney
aversion
certify
circulate
circumstance
commercial
concerted
conservative
conversion
currency

detergent
determine
deterrent
disconcerted
discourage
eternal
excursion
exterminate
furniture
germinate
hernia
hurricane
impertinence
impervious

internal
interpret
inversion
maternal
nocturnal
paternal
percolate
perforate
permanent
perpetrate
persecute
pertinent
refurbish
rehearsal   ►

ɝ IN WORDS OF THREE OR MORE SYLLABLES (*CONTINUED*)

◄

res**ur**gence	sup**er**lative	t**ur**bulence
rev**er**sal	s**ur**rogate	t**ur**pentine
sub**ur**ban	t**er**minate	
sup**er**fluous	th**er**mostat	

ɚ IN TWO-SYLLABLE WORDS

-**ar** (*suffix*)	cell**ar**	don**or**
-**er** (*suffix*)	cens**ure**	eag**er**
-**or** (*suffix*)	cent**er**	eff**or**t
act**or**	chapt**er**	emb**er**
aft**er**	chatt**er**	ent**er**
alt**ar**	cid**er**	err**or**
alt**er**	ciph**er**	ev**er**
amb**er**	clatt**er**	exp**er**t
anch**or**	clev**er**	fact**or**
ang**er**	clos**ure**	falt**er**
answ**er**	clust**er**	farth**er**
arb**or**	clutt**er**	fath**er**
ard**or**	coll**ar**	fav**or**
arm**or**	col**or**	feath**er**
auth**or**	comf**or**t	feat**ure**
awkw**ar**d	conc**er**t (*noun*)	ferment
bann**er**	conqu**er**	fig**ure**
bart**er**	coug**ar**	filt**er**
bett**er**	count**er**	fing**er**
bick**er**	cov**er**	fixt**ure**
bitt**er**	crack**er**	flatt**er**
blend**er**	crat**er**	flav**or**
blist**er**	cult**ure**	flutt**er**
blund**er**	curtail	forget
bord**er**	dang**er**	forgive
broth**er**	daught**er**	fut**ure**
butch**er**	des**er**t (*noun*)	gath**er**
butt**er**	diff**er**	gend**er**
camph**or**	dinn**er**	gest**ure**
cand**or**	doct**or**	ging**er**
cat**er**	doll**ar**	glam**our**

►

◄ glimmer
glitter
grammar
hammer
hamper
hanger
harbor
hinder
honor
horror
humor
hunger
insert (*noun*)
intern
juncture
junior
juror
ladder
leader
leather
lecture
ledger
letter
limber
linger
litter
luster
manner
martyr
master
matter
meager
member
mentor
meter
minor
mixture
modern
moisture

molar
monster
mother
motor
mustard
nature
neither
never
odor
order
other
pamper
paper
partner
pasture
pattern
pepper
perfect (*verb*)
perform
perfume (*verb*)
perhaps
persist
persuade
pertain
picture
pillar
pitcher
plaster
platter
pleasure
poker
polar
ponder
posture
powder
power
pressure
proper
prosper

puncture
pursue
rather
razor
render
research (*noun*)
roster
rupture
sailor
scatter
scholar
scissors
sculpture
seizure
senior
shelter
shepherd
shoulder
shudder
shutter
silver
simmer
singer
sister
slander
slaughter
slender
smolder
smother
solar
soldier
spider
splatter
splendor
sponsor
stammer
stature
stranger
structure ►

ɚ IN TWO-SYLLABLE WORDS (*CONTINUED*)

◄

stubborn	taper	timber
suffer	teacher	traitor
sugar	temper	transfer (*noun*)
summer	tender	treasure
super	tenure	trigger
surmise	terror	tutor
surprise	texture	ulcer
survey (*verb*)	theater	usher
tailor	thunder	utter
tamper	tiger	western

ɚ IN WORDS OF THREE OR MORE SYLLABLES

administrator	confirmation	intercede
adventure	consider	intercept
adversary	contractor	intermediate
advertise	contributor	intermission
advisor	conversation	international
affirmation	creditor	interview
altercation	customer	investor
alternate	December	jeopardize
alveolar	decipher	manufacture
amateur	deliver	meander
ambassador	departure	mediator
ancestor	diameter	mediocre
appetizer	director	messenger
asunder	disaster	minister
bachelor	employer	misdemeanor
benefactor	enamored	muscular
bifurcate	encounter	nuclear
calculator	energy	observation
calendar	engender	officer
carpenter	entertain	overture
character	exercise	particular
chiropractor	expenditure	passenger
circulation	exterior	peculiar
composure	familiar	percentage
conference	hibernate	perceptible

►

◄ perfunctory   professor   signature
permission   property   similar
perpetual   prosecutor   singular
perspective   recover   sinister
philosopher   register   spectacular
photographer   regular   spectator
popular   remember   surveillance
posterior   repercussion   together
predecessor   secular   ulterior
preference   semester   vinegar
procedure   September   yesterday

Sentences: ɝ vs. ɚ

CD
29

Turn to CD Track 29. Listen to the recording of the following sentences, then read the sentences aloud. Concentrate on the pronunciation of the ɝ and ɚ sounds, which are marked phonetically.

1 The ambassador affirmed closure on the barter.

2 Herbert had a perceptible aversion to altercations.

3 Both actors and singers performed with purpose at the gathering.

4 Peter's awkward answer concerned investors.

5 He was disturbed by certain urban odors.

6 Do you perceive earthy colors to be particularly comforting?

7 I'm perturbed by a surge in perfunctory performances in theater.

8 Laverne yearned for an energizing herbal dessert.

9 The intern immersed herself in further research.

10 Stay alert and discerning to avoid disasters.

11 Tickets to the popular circus can be purchased this Thursday.

12 I am eager to exercise in the refurbished modern gym.

13 Birds chirped as they perched on the corner of the arbor.

14 Did you confirm the dinner reservations on Saturday?

15 The scholar felt pressured to pursue worthy work.

16 Her allergic reaction to camphor triggered a fever.

17 Kirsten has two older sisters and a younger brother.

18 The leaders of yesterday's merger pledged a better use of power.

19 Do professors remember the days of registering for September semesters?

20 My cat Ferguson purrs with pleasure on sunny summer afternoons.

THIRTEEN

The vowel ʌ

The ʌ sound defined

The short *u* sound, represented by the phonetic symbol ʌ (as in *puddle*), is almost always mispronounced by nonnative speakers of English. It is usually replaced by the vowel ɑ (as in *pasta*). This is an understandable mistake, since ɑ is found in nearly all languages and ʌ is used almost exclusively in English. These two vowel sounds are made very close to each other, but with a definite change in the arch of the tongue from one to the other.

For both sounds, the tip of the tongue is resting against the lower teeth. But ʌ is a middle vowel, with a distinct arch in the middle of the tongue. By contrast, ɑ is a back vowel, occurring farther back in the mouth. In addition, ɑ is the only English vowel where the tongue has no arch but remains flat on the floor of the mouth.

Correcting the ʌ/ɑ vowel substitution can be easy, once one learns the difference in their tongue placements. It is also easy to recognize which of the two should be used by remembering a spelling pattern formula: ʌ is usually spelled with *u* (as in *bus, cup,* and *judge*) and sometimes with *o* (as in *mother, one,* and *love*), while ɑ is usually spelled with *o* (as in *honest, bond,* and *rock*), although there is a small number of words that are pronounced with ɑ and are spelled with *a* (as in *father, drama,* and *pasta*).

Let's pause for a moment and take a deep breath—this is not as confusing as it sounds. True, we have just entered the mysterious world of the *o* spelling pattern, a shining example of the lack of logic in the correspondence between pronunciation and spelling in the English language. But there is a trick here that you can use to distinguish between ʌ and ɑ: Just look at the word lists in this chapter. All the common words in English that use an *o* spelling pattern and are pronounced with ʌ are found in the "ʌ with *o* spelling" lists in this chapter. If a word spelled with *o* is not on one of these lists, it is either pronounced with ɑ or with the diphthong oŭ, which is addressed in Chapter Sixteen. And all the common words in English that are pronounced with ʌ—either with an *o* or *u* spelling pattern—are in the word lists in this chapter.

Now, let's turn our attention to the difference in the physical placements of ʌ and ɑ.

Step 1: Feeling the placement of ʌ

DVD
11

*Turn now to **DVD Track 11**,* where a step-by-step demonstration of the difference between ʌ and ɑ is presented. After you have watched the DVD, read the following description of the sound placements and do the exercises below.

Take out your mirror. Begin by saying ɑ, since you already pronounce this sound correctly. Say the word *ah* several times. Looking in the mirror, become aware of your tongue's placement. Notice that the tip of your tongue is resting against your lower teeth and the entire body of your tongue is lying flat on the floor of your mouth. You can check yourself by placing the tip of your little finger on the top edge of your lower teeth, as demonstrated on the DVD. Feel that there is no arch in your tongue against your finger as you say *ah*.

Now, keeping the tip of your tongue against your lower teeth, let the middle of your tongue arch forward about one-quarter inch against your finger. This is the placement of the vowel ʌ, as in *up*. Move back and forth between these two vowel positions: ɑ . . . ʌ . . . ɑ . . . ʌ.

*Return now to **DVD Track 11**.* Practice the difference in placement between the sounds ʌ and ɑ.

Step 2: Hearing the placement of ʌ

Using the mirror, look closely inside your mouth. Move your tongue back and forth between the placements of these two words: *ah . . . up . . . ah . . . up . . . ah . . . up . . . ah . . . up.* (Of course, your lips will come together for the consonant p.)

Watch in the mirror as you pronounce the pairs of words in the following lists. Listen to the differences between ʌ and ɑ, so that you can train your ear to hear the distinction, as well as feel the physiological difference in placement.

ʌ WITH *u* SPELLING	ɑ WITH *a* SPELLING
f<u>u</u>n	f<u>a</u>ther
pl<u>u</u>g	p<u>a</u>sta
dr<u>u</u>m	dr<u>a</u>ma

ʌ WITH *u* SPELLING	ɑ WITH *o* SPELLING
b<u>u</u>t	b<u>o</u>tch
p<u>u</u>ff	p<u>o</u>llen
s<u>u</u>dden	s<u>o</u>ck
t<u>u</u>mble	T<u>o</u>m
cl<u>u</u>tch	cl<u>o</u>ck
ch<u>u</u>ckle	ch<u>o</u>p
th<u>u</u>nder	thr<u>o</u>ttle
r<u>u</u>b	r<u>o</u>b
h<u>u</u>t	h<u>o</u>t
p<u>u</u>n	p<u>o</u>nder
c<u>u</u>lture	c<u>o</u>lumn
n<u>u</u>t	n<u>o</u>t

ʌ WITH *o* SPELLING	ɑ WITH *o* SPELLING
m<u>o</u>ther	m<u>o</u>nster
br<u>o</u>ther	br<u>o</u>th
<u>o</u>ther	h<u>o</u>nest
fl<u>oo</u>d	f<u>o</u>nd
t<u>o</u>ngue	t<u>o</u>ngs

CD

30

Turn now to **CD Track 30,** which features the sound adjustments between ʌ and ɑ. Repeat the pairs of words, while comparing your pronunciation with that on the CD.

Record your own pronunciation, and compare it to the CD track. Repeat this exercise until you feel ready to proceed to the next step.

Step 3: Applying the placement of ʌ

Following are lists of common English words that contain the ʌ sound. You can practice this sound by reading these lists aloud. After you have mastered the sound, advance to the sentences in the next section.

ʌ WITH *O, Oe, OO,* OR *OU* SPELLING IN ONE-SYLLABLE WORDS

blood	monk	son
come	month	sponge
does	none	ton
done	of	tongue
dove	once	touch
flood	one	tough*
from	rough*	won
front	shove	young
glove	slough*	
love	some	

ʌ WITH *O* OR *OU* SPELLING IN TWO-SYLLABLE WORDS

above	confront	enough*
affront	country	frontier
among	couple	govern
become	cousin	honey
beloved	cover	hover
brother	covet	income
color	doesn't	London
comfort	double	Monday
compass	dozen	money ►

*When the *gh* spelling pattern occurs at the end of a syllable or word, it is often pronounced f.

◄ monkey retouch somewhere
mother shovel southern
nothing smother stomach
onion somehow trouble
other someone wonder
outcome something youngster
oven sometimes
pommel somewhat

ʌ WITH O SPELLING IN WORDS OF THREE OR MORE SYLLABLES

accompanist coverage nobody
accompany discomfort otherwise
another discover overcome
anyone everybody recover
brotherhood everyone slovenly
comfortable governess somebody
comforter government wonderful
company governor wondrous

ʌ WITH U SPELLING IN ONE-SYLLABLE WORDS

bluff bump crumb*
blunt bun crunch
blush bunch crush
brunt bunk crust
brush bunt crutch
brusque bus cub
buck bust cuff
bud but cult
budge butt cup
buff buzz cusp
bug chuck cut
bulb chunk drug
bulge club drum
bulk clump drunk
bum clutch duck ►

---

*When the *mb* spelling pattern occurs at the end of a syllable or word, the *b* is silent and not pronounced.

A WITH *u* SPELLING IN ONE-SYLLABLE WORDS (*CONTINUED*)

◄ duct	hug	nub
dug	huh	nudge
dull	hulk	null
dumb*	hull	numb*
dump	hum	nun
dusk	hump	nut
dust	hunch	pluck
Dutch	hung	plug
fluff	hunk	plum
flung	hunt	plump
flunk	hush	plunge
flush	husk	plus
flux	hut	plush
fudge	judge	pub
fun	jug	puff
fund	jump	pulp
funk	junk	pulse
fuss	just	pump
fuzz	luck	pun
glum	lug	punch
glut	lull	punk
grudge	lump	punt
gruff	lunch	pup
grunt	lung	rub
gulf	lush	rug
gull	lust	rum
gulp	much	run
gum	mud	rung
gun	mug	runt
gush	mulch	rush
gust	mull	rust
gut	mumps	rut
hub	musk	scrub
huff	must	scruff ►

---

*When the *mb* spelling pattern occurs at the end of a syllable or word, the *b* is silent and not pronounced.

◄
scrunch	snug	sun
scuff	sprung	sung
sculpt	spud	sunk
scum	spun	swum
shrub	spunk	swung
shrug	struck	thrush
shrunk	strum	thrust
shun	strung	thud
shush	stub	thug
shut	stuck	thumb*
skull	stud	thump
skunk	stuff	thus
sludge	stump	truck
slug	stun	trunk
slum	stung	trust
slump	stunt	tub
slung	sub	tuck
slush	such	tug
smudge	suck	tusk
smug	sulk	up
snub	sum	us

ʌ WITH *u* SPELLING IN TWO-SYLLABLE WORDS

abrupt	buckle	chuckle
adjunct	buddy	clumsy
adult	budget	cluster
afflux	bundle	clutter
annul	bungle	conduct
begun	bunny	construct
blubber	bustle	consult
bludgeon	butler	corrupt
blunder	butter	crumble
bluster	button	culprit
bubble	buzzard	culture
bucket	chubby	cunning

►

*When the *mb* spelling pattern occurs at the end of a syllable or word, the *b* is silent and not pronounced.

Λ WITH *u* SPELLING IN TWO-SYLLABLE WORDS (*CONTINUED*)

◄

custom	judgment	rubber
defunct	juggle	rubbish
discuss	jumble	rubble
disgust	jumbo	rudder
disrupt	junction	ruffle
distrust	juncture	rugby
divulge	jungle	rumble
duchess	justice	rummage
dulcet	knuckle	rumple
dungeon	kumquat	runner
erupt	lumber	rupture
expunge	luscious	Russia
exult	muddle	rustic
fluster	muffin	rustle
flutter	mumble	scrumptious
frustrate	muscle	scuffle
fumble	muslin	sculpture
function	mustache	scuttle
fungus	mustard	shudder
funnel	muster	shuffle
funny	mutter	shutter
grumble	number	shuttle
grumpy	nuzzle	slumber
gusto	obstruct	smuggle
gutter	occult	snuggle
huddle	plunder	sputter
Hudson	public	structure
humble	publish	struggle
hundred	puddle	stubble
hunger	pulsate	stubborn
hungry	pumpkin	study
hunter	pundit	stumble
husband	punish	subject (*noun*)
hustle	puppet	sublet
impulse	puzzle	substance
indulge	refund	substrate
influx	repulse	subtle
insult	result	suburb

►

◀ subway
suction
sudden
suffer
suffix
sulfate
sulfur
sullen
sultry
summer
summit
summon
sundae
Sunday
sunny
supper

supple
surplus
suspect (*noun*)
thunder
trumpet
truncate
tumble
tunnel
tussle
ugly
ulcer
ultra
umbrage
umpire
uncle
under

unction
upgrade
uplift
upper
upright
uproar
upset
upside
upstairs
uptown
upward
utter
vulgar
vulture

ʌ WITH *u* SPELLING IN WORDS OF THREE OR MORE SYLLABLES

abundance
accustom
adjustment
agriculture
assumption
asunder
autumnal
avuncular
befuddle
buffalo
Columbia
combustible
compulsion
compulsive
conductor
conjunction
construction
consumption
cucumber
culminate
cumbersome

custody
customer
deduction
destruction
difficult
discussion
ebullient
enunciate
exculpatory
expulsion
filibuster
fluctuate
fundamental
gullible
illustrious
incumbent
induction
industrial
industrious
injunction
instruction

interrupt
introduction
jugular
justification
justify
luxury
multiple
mushroom
nullification
nullify
penultimate
percussion
perfunctory
production
productive
profundity
pronunciation
publication
publicity
pulmonary
pulverize ▶

Λ WITH *u* SPELLING IN WORDS OF THREE OR MORE SYLLABLES (*CONTINUED*)

◄ pumpernickel   resuscitate   triumphant

pumpernickel	resuscitate	triumphant
punctual	seduction	truculence
punctuate	subjectivity	tumultuous
punctuation	submarine	ulterior
punishment	subsequent	ultimate
rambunctious	subsidize	ultimatum
reduction	substantive	umbilical
redundant	substitute	umbrella
reluctance	substitution	upbringing
renunciation	suffocate	upheaval
repercussion	summarize	upside-down
reproduction	summary	utterly
republic	supplement	vulnerable
republican	supposition	
repugnance	sustenance	

Note: The *un-* prefix, as in *unable* and *undefeated,* is always pronounced with Λ.

EXCEPTIONS: Λ WITH *a* SPELLING

was	whatever
wasn't	
what	

Sentences: Λ

Turn to **CD Track 31.** Listen to the recording of the following sentences, then read the sentences aloud. Concentrate on correctly pronouncing the Λ sound, which is marked phonetically.

CD
31

1 My uncle hosted a luscious brunch on Sunday, with fun company.

2 Her brother recovered almost nothing after the destruction from the flood.

3 Everybody loves a sunny vacation at a southern country club.

4 Justin justified multiple deductions on his income tax and got

   a large sum for a refund.

5 Tension in the tongue muscle can be an obstruction to wonderful

   pronunciation.

6 Bud confronted a couple of frustrating and brusque customers.

7 Mushrooms and onions were baked in the oven with a crumbly,

   buttery crust.

8 Monday morning comes much too early after a weekend deadline

   crunch.

9 Dulcet music accompanied the otherwise utterly jarring percussion.

10 An abundance of love and money made Chuck a lucky young sculptor.

11 Another impulsive assumption turned our plans asunder.

12 Eating junk food always upsets my stomach.

13 The stunt driver plunged the car into the Hudson River.

14 She was repulsed by his enormous consumption of fudge.

15 A sudden rambunctious clamor erupted from the drunken crowd.

16 Who among us doesn't fundamentally prefer comfort?

17 Whatever would compel Judd to put mustard on his muffin?

18 He ordered a dozen fresh pumpernickel buns and some plum jelly.

19 The cold g(∧)ust (∧)of wind on the s(∧)ubway platform w(∧)as n(∧)umbing.

20 S(∧)omehow, D(∧)ustin adj(∧)usted to the reperc(∧)ussions fr(∧)om the tum(∧)ultuous scene.

Sentences: ∧ vs. ɑ

Turn to **CD Track 32**. Listen to the recording of the following sentences, then read the sentences aloud. Concentrate on distinguishing between the ∧ and ɑ sounds, which are marked phonetically.

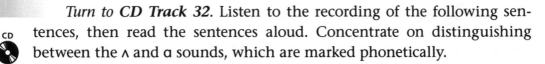

CD

32

1 F(ɑ)athers and m(∧)others are s(ɑ)ometimes at (ɑ)odds over when to ind(∧)ulge

   y(∧)oungsters.

2 Having a n(∧)umber (∧)of pr(ɑ)oblems to s(ɑ)olve kept f(∧)un-l(∧)oving J(ɑ)ohn

   (∧)out (∧)of tr(∧)ouble.

3 A surpl(∧)us (∧)of spending is (ɑ)often disc(∧)overed when f(ɑ)ollow-(∧)up b(∧)udgets

   are d(∧)one.

4 Constr(∧)uction (ɑ)on the d(ɑ)octor's (ɑ)office w(∧)as abr(∧)uptly disr(∧)upted this m(∧)onth.

5 The s(∧)ummer s(∧)un w(∧)as str(ɑ)ong and unc(∧)omf(∧)ortably h(ɑ)ot.

6 When fr(ɑ)ost is (ɑ)on the p(ɑ)ond, b(∧)utton (∧)up and wear gl(∧)oves.

7 Any(∧)one can bec(∧)ome t(∧)ongue-tied when c(ɑ)onstantly c(ɑ)ontradicted.

8 He ins(∧)ulted D(ɑ)onna by disc(∧)ussing her level (∧)of c(ɑ)ompetence (ɑ)on the pr(ɑ)oject.

9 The l(ɑ)ong, (∧)upbeat r(ɑ)ock s(ɑ)ong w(∧)as (∧)uplifting.

10 I have a h(∧)unch that a pr(ɑ)ompt resp(ɑ)onse would be prod(∧)uctive.

11 Subsequent subsidies would help recover operating costs.

12 Bonnie shopped compulsively for comfortable socks.

13 A combination of condiments made the otherwise dull dish

scrumptious.

14 The holiday season made Molly feel nostalgic and vulnerable.

15 We must acknowledge the loss of lost cultures.

16 Multiple interruptions prompted Collin to shush his colleagues.

17 Can we have a discussion about common misconduct with customers?

18 My brother sometimes divulges controversial gossip.

19 Take the polished document of summarized instructions into

the conferences.

20 Turn obstinate reluctance into positive optimism!

FOURTEEN

The vowel ʊ

Fred was now well established at the securities firm, and he was entrusted with the enviable task of signing a lucrative new account over an extensive and expensive business lunch. His client remarked that the portions were huge and that she was so full from her entrée that she couldn't even consider having dessert. As the waiter began to recite the list of rich chocolate pastries available, Fred politely interrupted. "She doesn't want dessert," he announced, shaking his head. "She's fool."

The ʊ sound defined

The *oo* sound, represented by the phonetic symbol ʊ (as in *full*), is often confused with the sound u (as in *fool*). As with other vowel sounds in English that cause confusion for nonnative speakers, the reason is that ʊ is used almost exclusively in English, whereas u is found in nearly all languages. Both vowel sounds are made close together, but with a slight difference in the arch of the tongue and a marked difference in lip rounding.

Both u and ʊ are back vowels: The tip of the tongue is resting against the lower teeth and it is the arch in the back of the tongue that determines the vowels' sounds. The difference in placement of the arch of the tongue is minuscule—about one-eighth of an inch. However, u has a much more noticeable lip rounding than ʊ.

Correcting the u/ʊ vowel substitution can be easy, once you learn the difference in tongue placement and how to relax your lips. However, it is difficult to tell which vowel sound is pronounced by spelling pattern alone; both sounds are commonly associated with *oo, ou,* and *u* spellings. The good news is that ʊ is not frequently used in English. The word lists in this chapter contain all the common English words that have the ʊ sound. By becoming familiar with these words, you will easily recognize when to use this vowel.

Step 1: Feeling the placement of ʊ

DVD

12

Turn now to **DVD Track 12**, where a step-by-step demonstration of the differences between u and ʊ is presented. After you have watched the DVD, read the following description of the sound placement and do the exercises below.

Take out your mirror. Begin by saying u, since you already pronounce this sound correctly. Say the word *who* several times. Looking in the mirror, become aware of the placement of both your tongue and your lips. Notice that the tip of your tongue is resting against your lower teeth and that the back of your tongue is arched forward. You can check yourself by placing the tip of your little finger on the top edge of your lower teeth, as demonstrated on the DVD. Feel the arch in the back of your tongue as it contacts your finger when you say *who.* Also, feel your lips rounded around your finger.

Return your tongue to its resting position, with the tip of your tongue resting against your lower teeth, but with the body of your tongue lying flat on the floor of your mouth. Say the word *who* again, freezing on the vowel. Once again, you will feel the arch of your tongue contact the tip of your finger and your lips rounded around your finger.

Now, drop the arch of your tongue backward about one-eighth of an inch, leaving the tip of your tongue against your lower teeth. Relax your lips by releasing the tension in the inner lip muscle. Looking in the mirror, notice that there is still a slight rounding on the outside of the lips, but that the inner lip muscle relaxes considerably. This is the placement of the vowel ʊ, as in *hood*. Go back and forth between these two placements: u...ʊ...u...ʊ.

*Return now to **DVD Track 12**.* Practice the difference in placement between the sounds u and ʊ.

Step 2: Hearing the placement of ʊ

Using the mirror, look closely inside your mouth. Move your tongue back and forth between the placements of these two words: *who ... hood ... who ... hood ... who ... hood ... who ... hood.* (Of course, the tip of your tongue will touch the alveolar ridge for the consonant d.)

Watch in the mirror as you pronounce the pairs of words in the following list. Listen to the differences between u and ʊ, so that you can train your ear to hear the distinction, as well as feel the physiological difference in placement.

u	ʊ
boo	book
pool	pull
sue	soot
two	took
crew	could
shoe	should
route	rookie
fool	full
food	foot
brood	brook
cool	cook
stew	stood
lose	look

*Turn now to **CD Track 33**,* which features the sound adjustments between u and ʊ. Repeat the pairs of words, while comparing your pronunciation with that on the CD.

Record your own pronunciation, and compare it to the CD track. Repeat this exercise until you feel ready to proceed to the next step.

Step 3: Applying the placement of ʊ

Following are lists of all the common English words that contain the ʊ sound. Read through the lists carefully, and try to become familiar with these words. To choose between u and ʊ in pronouncing a word, refer to these lists; if the word is not listed here, it is safe to assume that the pronunciation uses u. You can practice the ʊ sound by reading these lists aloud. After you have mastered the sound, advance to the sentences in the next section.

ʊ IN ONE-SYLLABLE WORDS

-ful (*suffix*)*	good	shook
book	hood	should
brook	hoof	soot
bull	hook	stood
bush	look	took
cook	nook	wolf
could	pull	wood
crook	push	wool
foot	put	would
full	rook	

ʊ IN TWO-SYLLABLE WORDS

ambush	bookmark	bulldog
barefoot	bookshelf	bulldoze
bookcase	bookstore	bullet
bookend	bookworm	bullion
bookie	bosom	bully
booking	boyhood	bureau
booklet	Brooklyn	bushel ►

*The *u* of the suffix *-ful* is pronounced ʊ when the word is a noun, as in *cupful*. It is pronounced ə when the word is an adjective, as in *beautiful*.

◄ butcher
childhood
cookbook
cookie
couldn't
crooked
cushion
duress
during
euro
Europe
footage
football
footnote
footprint
footstep
Fulbright

fulcrum
fulfill
full-time
fury
goodbye
goodness
hoodlum
hoodwink
hoorah
input
juror
jury
lurid
mistook
mural
outlook
output

partook
pudding
pulley
pulpit
rookie
rural
shouldn't
sugar
tourist
unhook
urine
withstood
woman
wooden
woofer
woolen
wouldn't

ʊ IN WORDS OF THREE OR MORE SYLLABLES

assurance
bookkeeper
bulletin
cum laude
curiosity
durability
durable
duration
endurance
fulminate
furious

Hollywood
infuriate
injury
insurance
jurisdiction
luxurious
neighborhood
overlook
prurient
purification
purify

puritanical
purity
security
tourism
tournament
understood
uranium
Uranus
urinary
womanhood
curious

Sentences: ʊ

CD

34

*Turn to **CD Track 34**.* Listen to the recording of the following sentences, then read the sentences aloud. Concentrate on correctly pronouncing the ʊ sound, which is marked phonetically.

1 It would be good to treat your books with care to increase their durability.

2 Anthony took a luxurious full-time position as a tourist in Europe.

3 The woman put extra sugar in the cookie and pudding recipes.

4 I'm curious—did you have the butcher's assurance of the meat's purity?

5 The coach shouldn't have pushed the rookie football player during training.

6 An enticing bull market can make many investors overlook good judgment.

7 The Brooklyn attorney hoped the jury understood his argument.

8 The earthquake shook the buildings furiously, but they withstood the rocking.

9 Pull up the hood of your raincoat during a storm—it actually enhances the look.

10 The cook used wooden stakes to anchor the herb bushes.

11 My bookcase is full of overlooked books.

12 Are wooden clogs really good for a foot?

13 In childhood, did you read of Red Riding Hood and the wolf?

14 The woman's outlook was off-putting and arrogant.

15 Fortunately, he bought full insurance before his injury.

16 The rookie was a hoodlum and a crook.

17 Look at the mural—does it look crooked?

18 When the fulcrum cracked, the pulley could no longer be used.

19 I love the look of wool sweaters with wooden buttons.

20 The bookie took heavy bets during football season.

Sentences: ʊ vs. u

Turn to CD Track 35. Listen to the recording of the following sentences, then read the sentences aloud. Concentrate on distinguishing between the ʊ and u sounds, which are marked phonetically.

1 Julie understood her full-time nanny couldn't be booked during the month of June.

2 Who knew the cooking school's cookbooks couldn't be ordered until Tuesday?

3 In the dimly lit room, Drew mistook the new deep shade of blue for maroon.

4 You are confused: Brooklyn is not a rural environment infused with woods.

5 The jury took the duration of the afternoon to regroup and peruse the evidence.

6 I could use either cookies or pudding; any sugar buzz will do!

7 You should have learned in school that Uranus is a distant planet.

8 The wind blew furiously through the woods, pushing all the drooping bushes aside.

9 The woman proved to the group of youths that the bulldog by the pool was friendly.

10 Walking barefoot by the brook could be foolish. Put on shoes or boots.

11 You couldn't find a solution—or you wouldn't?

12 The woman shouldn't wear her new boots in June.

13 Did Ruth say goodbye when she left for the university in Europe?

14 I could use input on planning the school's tournament.

15 Would you like purified water or fruit juice?

16 The bulletin was full of good news about the youths.

17 I'm curious if Luke could pass a brutal endurance test.

18 The jurors felt duress in reaching a conclusion by the afternoon.

19 Tourism in Brooklyn has hugely improved in the last two decades.

20 The bully was infuriated when sent to school in June.

FIFTEEN

The vowel ɔ

The ɔ sound defined

The *au* or *aw* sound is represented by the phonetic symbol ɔ (as in *law*). Nonnative speakers of English often confuse this sound with the diphthong aŭ (as in *loud*). This is understandable, since the spelling patterns for ɔ are usually comprised of two vowels, and nonnative speakers assume that a phonetic relationship exists between the spelling of a word and its pronunciation. Unfortunately, English is not a phonetic language, as we've seen in previous chapters: Its spelling patterns often do not correspond to pronunciation. The phoneme ɔ is a pure vowel. A diphthong, as defined earlier, is a blend of two vowels sounded together as one. There is no diphthong in the pronunciation of ɔ, and therefore, the articulators do not move during the production of the sound.

The vowel ɔ is a back vowel: The tip of the tongue is resting against the lower teeth and it is the arch in the back of the tongue that determines its sound.

Correcting the tendency to diphthongize this vowel can be easy, once one realizes that the correct placement of ɔ involves no movement down the center axis of the lips. The spelling patterns for this sound are *a(l), au, aw, oa(d),* and *ou(gh)*. The word lists in this chapter contain all the common words in English that have the ɔ sound. By memorizing these spelling patterns and becoming familiar with the words in the lists, you will easily recognize when to use this vowel.

Step 1: Feeling the placement of ɔ

DVD

13

*Turn now to **DVD Track 13**, where a step-by-step demonstration of the difference between ɔ and aʊ is presented. After you have watched the DVD, read the following description of the sound placement and do the exercises below.

Take out your mirror. Begin by saying the aʊ sound, since you already pronounce this diphthong correctly. Say the word *loud* several times. Looking in the mirror, become aware of the placement of your tongue and lips. Notice that the tip of your tongue is resting against your lower teeth and that the back of your tongue arches forward during the movement of the diphthong. (Of course, your tongue will contact the alveolar ridge on both the l and d sounds.) You can check yourself by placing the tip of your little finger on the top edge of your lower teeth, as demonstrated on the DVD. Feel the arch in your tongue shift from the front to the back as you combine the two vowel sounds into the diphthong aʊ.

Even more importantly, notice that your lips round during the production of this sound. Put your index finger to your lips, as demonstrated on the DVD. Say the word *loud* several times, and while you watch in the mirror, feel your lips tighten down their center axis, against your index finger. There is distinct, marked lip rounding when forming this diphthong.

Return your tongue to its resting position, with the tip of your tongue against your lower teeth, but with the body of your tongue lying flat on the floor of your mouth. Say the word *loud* again, freezing at the end of the diphthong. Once again, feel with your index finger that your lips have rounded forward, with tension down their center axis.

Now, lower your jaw and relax your lips. Leaving the tip of your tongue against your lower teeth, allow your lips to form an oval shape, with a slight tension in the corners. Place the thumb and index finger of your right hand against the corners of your lips. Say the word *law*, using your index finger and thumb to "pull" the sound forward.

Refer again to the DVD and repeat this movement, following the on-screen instruction. This establishes the position of your outer lip muscles for the vowel ɔ.

The task now becomes to not move the center lip muscles during the production of the pure vowel ɔ. Place your index finger on the center axis of your lips again, and repeat the word *law*. Do not allow any movement down the center of your lips.

This is the placement of the vowel ɔ. Go back and forth between the two placements of aʊ and ɔ: aʊ . . . ɔ . . . aʊ . . . ɔ.

Return now to **DVD Track 13.** Practice the difference in placement between the diphthong aʊ and the vowel ɔ.

Step 2: Hearing the placement of ɔ

Using the mirror, look closely at your lips. Move your lips back and forth between the placements of these two words: *loud . . . law . . . loud . . . law . . . loud . . . law . . . loud . . . law.* (Of course, your tongue will touch the alveolar ridge for the consonants l and d.)

Watch in the mirror as you pronounce the pairs of words in the following list. Listen to the differences between aʊ and ɔ, so that you can train your ear to hear the distinction, as well as feel the physiological difference in placement.

aʊ	ɔ
bow	bought
crowd	call
round	raw
found	fall
ground	gall
brown	broad
pound	pause
town	tall
loud	law
power	paw
sour	saw
tower	taught
shower	shawl

CD
36

Turn now to CD Track 36, which features the sound adjustments between aŭ and ɔ. Repeat the pairs of words, while comparing your pronunciation with that on the CD.

Record your own pronunciation, and compare it to the CD track. Repeat this exercise until you feel ready to proceed to the next step.

Step 3: Applying the placement of ɔ

Following are lists of all the common English words that contain the ɔ sound, grouped by spelling pattern. Read through the lists carefully, and try to become familiar with these words. To choose between aŭ and ɔ in pronouncing a word, refer to these lists, using the spelling pattern. You can practice the ɔ sound by reading these lists aloud. After you have mastered the sound, advance to the sentences in the next section.

ɔ WITH *a(l)* SPELLING IN ONE-SYLLABLE WORDS

all	gall	small
bald	hall	stalk*
balk*	halt	stall
ball	mall	talk*
call	malt	tall
chalk*	pall	walk*
fall	salt	wall
false	scald	waltz

ɔ WITH *a(l)* SPELLING IN TWO-SYLLABLE WORDS

almost	appall	caldron
alright	asphalt	enthrall
also	ballpark	exalt
altar	ballroom	eyeball
alter	balsa	falcon
although	Baltic	fallen
always	baseball	fallout

►

---

*When the *alk* spelling pattern occurs at the end of a syllable or word, the *l* is silent and not pronounced.

◄

falter	install	smaller
football	palsy	stalwart
forestall	paltry	wallet
hallway	recall	walnut
halter	sidewalk*	walrus

ɔ WITH *a(l)* SPELLING IN WORDS OF THREE OR MORE SYLLABLES

Albany	altercation	falsetto
albeit	alternant	falsify
alderman	alternate	installment
allover	alternative	overall
almighty	altogether	subaltern
already	appalling	talkative*
alteration	balsamic	unalterable
altercate	Baltimore	wallflower

ɔ WITH *au* SPELLING IN ONE-SYLLABLE WORDS

aught	gaunt	pause
caught	gauze	sauce
cause	haul	staunch
daub	haunt	taught
daunt	jaunt	taunt
fault	laud	taut
faun	launch	vault
flaunt	maul	vaunt
fraud	naught	
fraught	paunch	

ɔ WITH *au* SPELLING IN TWO-SYLLABLE WORDS

applaud	auction	auspice
applause	audit	austere
assault	augment	author
auburn	August	auto

►

---

*When the *alk* spelling pattern occurs at the end of a syllable or word, the *l* is silent and not pronounced.

ɔ WITH *au* SPELLING IN TWO-SYLLABLE WORDS (*CONTINUED*)

◄

autumn	exhaust	onslaught
because	faucet	pauper
caucus	gaudy	raucous
causal	haughty	saucepan
causing	jaundice	saucer
caustic	laundry	saucy
caution	maraud	saunter
cautious	maudlin	sausage
daughter	naughty	sauté
default	nausea	slaughter
distraught	nauseous	trauma

ɔ WITH *au* SPELLING IN WORDS OF THREE OR MORE SYLLABLES

astronaut	authority	causative
audacious	authorization	cauterize
audacity	authorize	debauchery
audible	authorship	fraudulence
audience	autism	hydraulic
audio	autobiography	inaudible
audition	autocracy	inaugural
auditorium	autocratic	inauguration
auditory	autograph	laudable
augmentation	automatic	nautical
auspicious	automaton	nautilus
Australia	automobile	paucity
Austria	autopsy	plausible
authentic	auxiliary	traumatic
authenticate	Caucasian	
authenticity	cauliflower	

ɔ WITH *aw* SPELLING IN ONE-SYLLABLE WORDS

awe	claw	drawl
bawl	crawl	drawn
brawl	dawn	fawn
brawn	draw	flaw

►

◄	gawk	pawn	sprawl
gnaw*	prawn	squaw
hawk	raw	squawk
jaw	saw	straw
law	scrawl	thaw
lawn	shawl	yawn
paw	slaw

ɔ WITH *aw* SPELLING IN TWO-SYLLABLE WORDS

awesome	drawing	tawdry
awful	lawsuit	tawny
awkward	outlaw	withdraw
awning	rawhide	withdrawn
bawdy	sawdust	
crawfish	scrawny	

ɔ WITH *aw* SPELLING IN WORDS OF THREE OR MORE SYLLABLES

strawberry
withdrawal

ɔ WITH *oa(d)* SPELLING

abroad	broaden
broad	Broadway
broadcast	

ɔ WITH *ou(gh)* SPELLING†

afterthought	fought	thought
bought	ought	trough‡
brought	oughtn't	wrought
cough‡	sought	

---

*When the *gn* spelling pattern occurs at the beginning of a syllable or word, the *g* is silent and not pronounced.

†When the *ought* spelling pattern occurs in a word, the *gh* is silent and not pronounced.

‡*Cough* and *trough* are the only two common English words where the spelling pattern *ough* is pronounced ɔf.

Sentences: ɔ

Turn to CD Track 37. Listen to the recording of the following sentences, then read the sentences aloud. Concentrate on correctly pronouncing the ɔ sound, which is marked phonetically.

1 Paul recalled an awkward ballroom dancing audition in August.

2 The powerful inauguration speech brought applause from all

 in the audience.

3 The robbery was an exhausting trauma for the raucous author.

4 The lawn was luscious, despite the awful August heat.

5 Paula loved drawing landscapes of foliage in autumn.

6 My daughter insists that the hallway to the vault is haunted.

7 Adding sausage to the sauce caused the dish to become too salty.

8 He bought the tools to install the audio system under the awning.

9 She had the gall to file a lawsuit after causing the altercation.

10 I thought I caught a cold because of the faulty heating.

11 The dripping faucet kept the exhausted traveler from falling asleep

 until nearly dawn.

12 The authorities at the auction determined that the painting was a fraud.

13 You ought to be cautious and pause at an intersection.

14 The haughty actress always thought she would be a Broadway star.

15 The <u>a</u>wesome <u>A</u>ustralian baseb<u>a</u>ll player hit a grand slam out of the

b<u>a</u>llpark.

16 The f<u>aw</u>n w<u>a</u>lked across the l<u>aw</u>n just before d<u>aw</u>n.

17 The str<u>aw</u>berry w<u>a</u>lnut s<u>au</u>ce c<u>au</u>sed S<u>au</u>l to feel n<u>au</u>seous.

18 <u>A</u>ll the B<u>a</u>ltimore baseb<u>a</u>ll fans found the Yankees app<u>a</u>lling.

19 The father and d<u>au</u>ghter w<u>a</u>ltzed while the wedding guests appl<u>au</u>ded

<u>au</u>dibly.

20 Traveling abr<u>oa</u>d <u>au</u>tomatically br<u>oa</u>dened P<u>au</u>la's th<u>ou</u>ghts.

Sentences: ɔ vs. aʊ

*Turn to **CD Track 38**. Listen to the recording of the following sentences, then read the sentences aloud. Concentrate on distinguishing between the ɔ and aʊ sounds, which are marked phonetically.

1 D<u>aw</u>n <u>a</u>lways f<u>ou</u>nd herself sl<u>ou</u>ching on the c<u>ou</u>ch after exh<u>au</u>sting

<u>au</u>ditions.

2 During the tax <u>au</u>dit, P<u>au</u>l s<u>aw</u> that he had to acc<u>ou</u>nt for his firm's

all<u>ow</u>ed spending.

3 The chef th<u>aw</u>ed ten <u>ou</u>nces of s<u>au</u>sage for ab<u>ou</u>t half an h<u>ou</u>r.

4 By n<u>ow</u>, Cl<u>au</u>dia's <u>au</u>thority all<u>ow</u>ed her adversaries no d<u>ou</u>bt as to her

<u>au</u>thenticity.

5   The astron<u>au</u>t f<u>ou</u>nd comfort in listening to s<u>ou</u>nd recordings before
    the space l<u>au</u>nch.

6   "Watch <u>ou</u>t!" P<u>au</u>l sh<u>ou</u>ted to the p<u>au</u>nchy taxicab driver during
    the tr<u>au</u>matic drive.

7   <u>Au</u>though he didn't lose the acc<u>ou</u>nt, S<u>au</u>l felt that his pitch was f<u>au</u>lty.

8   We f<u>ou</u>nd the ch<u>au</u>lk dr<u>awi</u>ng on the sidew<u>au</u>lk <u>ou</u>tside the h<u>ou</u>se
    to be <u>aw</u>esome!

9   The appl<u>au</u>se in the <u>au</u>ditorium c<u>au</u>sed the pr<u>ou</u>d actors to take
    a second b<u>ow</u>.

10 The <u>au</u>ctioneer th<u>ou</u>ght she <u>ou</u>ght to all<u>ow</u> the bidder to withdr<u>aw</u> n<u>ow</u>.

11 C<u>ou</u>nt on s<u>au</u>téed pr<u>aw</u>ns to be a cr<u>ow</u>d-pleaser.

12 No d<u>ou</u>bt L<u>au</u>ra will be gr<u>ou</u>nded when she's n<u>au</u>ghty.

13 I was <u>au</u>ready d<u>ow</u>nt<u>ow</u>n when I got the c<u>au</u>ll.

14 She had the <u>au</u>dacity to be pr<u>ou</u>d of c<u>au</u>sing a l<u>ou</u>d <u>au</u>tercation.

15 P<u>au</u>l h<u>ou</u>sed c<u>ow</u>s on his spr<u>aw</u>ling l<u>aw</u>ns.

16 The in<u>au</u>gural speech was <u>au</u>thoritative, p<u>ow</u>erful, and r<u>ou</u>sing.

17 <u>Au</u>ways use c<u>au</u>tion when car<u>ou</u>sing d<u>ow</u>n s<u>ou</u>th.

18 The cr<u>ow</u>d at the football game was r<u>ow</u>dy and r<u>au</u>cous.

19 I d<u>ou</u>bt you were t<u>au</u>ght to f<u>au</u>lsify your acc<u>ou</u>nting records.

20 I s<u>au</u>w a sm<u>au</u>ll t<u>ow</u>n ar<u>ou</u>nd the m<u>ou</u>ntain bend.

SIXTEEN

The vowels *a* and *oŏ*

The *a* and *oŏ* sounds defined

The *o* spelling pattern is usually mispronounced by nonnative speakers of English as a pure vowel represented by the phonetic symbol o. This sound is rarely used in English. In Chapter Thirteen, which treated the vowel ʌ, we entered the mysterious world of the *o* spelling pattern, a shining example of the lack of logic in the correspondence between English spelling and pronunciation.

There is, however, a trick that you can use to distinguish among the vowels ʌ, a, and oŏ. For all *o* spelling patterns, first check the word lists for ʌ with an *o* spelling pattern in Chapter Thirteen: All of the common English words that contain *o* pronounced as ʌ are found in Chapter Thirteen.

If a word containing *o* is not on one of those lists, it is pronounced either with a or with the diphthong oŏ, and all of the common words with an a or oŏ pronunciation are presented in the word lists in this chapter.

Step 1: Feeling the placement of *a* vs. *oŏ*

*Turn now to **DVD Track 14**,* where a step-by-step demonstration of the difference between a and oŏ is presented. After you have watched the DVD, read the following description of the sound placement and do the exercises below.

DVD
14

173

Take out your mirror. Begin by placing the tip of your tongue against your lower teeth. Now, place the tip of your little finger on your lower teeth so that it touches the front and middle of your tongue. Say u . . . ʊ . . . ɔ. You will feel the back of your tongue arch, dropping about one-eighth of an inch from one vowel to the next.

Now, drop your tongue until it is lying flat on the floor of your mouth, and completely relax your lips. This is the position for ɑ. Say ɑ, then say u . . . ʊ . . . ɔ . . . ɑ . . . u . . . ʊ . . . ɔ . . . ɑ. Next, say u . . . *who* . . . ʊ . . . *hood* . . . ɔ . . . *awesome*. Now, drop your tongue until it's lying flat, and say ɑ . . . *stop*.

Next, let's consider the diphthong oʊ̆. We will begin with the o sound, since you already pronounce this vowel correctly. Place the tip of your little finger between your lips, just outside your front teeth, and say o. You will feel your upper and lower lips touching your finger, and the inner lip muscles are fairly relaxed. Now, say ʊ. You will feel the inside of your lips rounding slightly. Say o . . . ʊ. Now, combine o and ʊ: oʊ̆ . . . oʊ̆ . . . oʊ̆.

Last, contrast the two *o* vowels: ɑ . . . oʊ̆ . . . ɑ . . . oʊ̆ . . . ɑ . . . oʊ̆.

Return now to **DVD Track 14**. Practice the difference in placement between the sounds ɑ and oʊ̆.

Step 2: Hearing the placement of *ɑ* vs. *oʊ̆*

Using the mirror, look closely at your mouth. Move your lips back and forth between the placements of these two words: *stop* . . . *go* . . . *stop* . . . *go* . . . *stop* . . . *go*. (Of course, your lips will come together for the consonant p.)

Watch in the mirror as you pronounce the pairs of words in the following list. Listen to the differences between ɑ and oʊ̆, so that you can train your ear to hear the distinction, as well as feel the physiological difference in placement.

ɑ	oʊ̆
ch<u>o</u>ck	ch<u>o</u>ke
cl<u>o</u>th	cl<u>o</u>the
c<u>o</u>p	c<u>o</u>pe
d<u>o</u>t	d<u>o</u>te
c<u>o</u>st	c<u>oa</u>st

►

a	o͝o
hop	hope
God	goat
not	note
rob	robe
strong	stroke
blot	both
lot	load

CD

39

Turn now to CD Track 39, which features the sound adjustments between a and o͝o. Repeat the pairs of words, while comparing your pronunciation with that on the CD.

Record your own pronunciation, and compare it to the CD track. Repeat this exercise until you feel ready to proceed to the next step.

Step 3: Applying the placement of *a* vs. *o͝o*

Following are lists of all the common English words that contain the a and o͝o sounds, grouped by spelling pattern. Read through the lists carefully, and try to become familiar with these words. To choose between a and o͝o in pronouncing a word, refer to these lists.

You can practice the a and o͝o sounds by reading these lists aloud. After you have mastered the sounds, advance to the sentences in the next section.

a WITH *a* SPELLING IN ONE-SYLLABLE WORDS

alms*	schwa	swap
balm*	shah	swat
calm*	spa	want
palm*	squad	wash
psalm*	squash	wasp
quad	suave	watch
qualm*	swamp	watt
quash	swan	yacht

---

*When the *alm* spelling pattern occurs at the end of a syllable or word, the *l* is silent and not pronounced.

ɑ WITH *a* SPELLING IN TWO-SYLLABLE WORDS

almond*	llama	quantum
barrage	mama	quarrel
collage	mamba	savant
corsage	massage	squabble
drama	mirage	squander
embalm*	nuance	swallow
façade	papa	waffle
father	pasta	wallet
garage	plaza	warrant
lava	quadrant	wander

ɑ WITH *a* SPELLING IN WORDS OF THREE OR MORE SYLLABLES

aria	iguana	quantity
camouflage	karate	renaissance
debacle	piranha	safari
debutant	pyjamas	sonata
enchilada	qualify	warrior
espionage	qualitative	Washington
finale	quality	

ɑ WITH *o* SPELLING IN ONE-SYLLABLE WORDS

blob	clock	dodge
block	clog	dog
blond	clot	doll
blot	cloth	dot
blotch	cog	drop
bomb	con	flock
boss	cop	flog
botch	cost	flop
Bronx	cot	floss
bronze	crock	fog
broth	crop	fond
chock	cross	font
chop	dock	fox ►

*When the *alm* spelling pattern occurs at the end of a syllable or word, the *l* is silent.

◄ frock   mock   scoff
frog   mop   shock
frost   moss   shop
gloss   moth   shot
God   nod   slob
golf   not   slot
gone   notch   smock
gong   odd   snob
hog   off   sob
honk   on   sock
hop   ox   soft
hot   plod   solve
job   plop   song
jog   plot   stock
jot   pomp   stomp
knob   pond   stop
knock   pop   strong
knot   pot   throb
lodge   prod   tongs
loft   prompt   top
log   prop   toss
long   rob   trod
loss   rock   trot
lost   rod   wrong
lot   romp
mob   rot

a WITH *o* SPELLING IN TWO-SYLLABLE WORDS

abscond   blossom   cobble
absolve   body   coddle
accost   boggle   coffee
across   bonnet   coffin
adopt   bother   cognate
aloft   bottle   collar
along   bottom   colleague
baton   chaos   collie
begot   chiffon   column
belong   chronic   combat (*noun*)
beyond   closet   comic   ►

a WITH o SPELLING IN TWO-SYLLABLE WORDS (*CONTINUED*)

◄

comma	devolve	modern
comment	diphthong	modest
commerce	dissolve	monarch
common	docile	monster
commune	doctor	nonsense
compact (*noun*)	doctrine	nostril
compound (*noun*)	dogma	novel
concave	dollar	novice
concept	dolphin	nozzle
concert (*noun*)	donkey	nylon
concourse	evolve	object (*noun*)
concrete (*noun*)	fodder	oblong
conduct (*noun*)	folly	offer
conflict (*noun*)	forgot	office
Congress	fossil	often
conquer	glottal	olive
conquest	gobble	option
conscience	goggle	ostrich
conscious	gospel	phosphate
constant	gossip	pocket
contact	hobble	polish
content (*noun*)	hobby	pollen
contest (*noun*)	hockey	pompous
context	homage	ponder
contour	honest	problem
contract (*noun*)	hostage	process
contrast (*noun*)	hostile	product
convent	icon	profit
convert (*noun*)	involve	progress (*noun*)
convex	jockey	project (*noun*)
convict (*noun*)	jolly	promise
convoy	jostle	proper
copper	knowledge	prospect
copy	lobby	prosper
costume	lobster	province
cottage	logic	resolve
cotton	lozenge	respond
coupon	model	response

►

◀   revolve   tonic   vodka
    roster   topple   volley
    solid   toxic   volume
    sorry   upon

a WITH *o* SPELLING IN WORDS OF THREE OR MORE SYLLABLES

-ocracy (*suffix*)	apothecary	cogitate
-ographer (*suffix*)	approximate	colony
-ography (*suffix*)	archeology	colossal
-ologer (*suffix*)	astonish	columnist
-ology (*suffix*)	astrology	combination
abdominal	astronomer	comedy
abolish	atomic	commentary
abominable	atrocity	commodity
accommodate	autocracy	communism
accomplice	automaton	comparable
accomplish	barometer	compensate
acknowledge	binoculars	competence
admonish	biographer	competition
agglomerate	biography	complicate
agnostic	biology	compliment
alcohol	bombastic	composite
analogue	botany	comprehend
anatomic	broccoli	compromise
androgynous	bronchial	concentrate
animosity	bureaucracy*	condescend
anomaly	cacophony	condiment
anonymous	cartography	condominium
anthology	chocolate	conference
anthropology	cholera	confidence
apocalypse	choreography	confiscate
apologize	chronically	conglomerate
apostle	chronology	congruous
apostrophe	cinematography	conjugate ▶

---

*This is an exception to the spelling patterns of *a*.

ɑ WITH O SPELLING IN WORDS OF THREE OR MORE SYLLABLES (*CONTINUED*)

◄

connotation	geology	monument
consecrate	harmonic	myopic
consequence	hexagon	narcotic
consolidate	histrionic	nocturnal
constitute	holiday	nominal
consultation	Hollywood	nominate
contemplate	homicide	nostalgia
contradict	homily	obfuscate
contradiction	homogenize	obligate
contrary	homonym	obnoxious
controversy	horrible	obstacle
convalesce	hospital	obstinate
conversation	hypnotic	obvious
convocation	hypocrisy	occupant
convolute	hypothesis	octagon
correspondence	ideology	octopus
correspondent	incomparable	opera
corroborate	innocuous	operate
cosmetic	insomnia	operative
cosmopolitan	interrogative	opportune
crocodile	ironic	opposite
curiosity	lottery	optimism
cytology	mahogany	optimum
democracy	mediocrity	ostensible
demolish	melancholy	oxidize
deposit	metabolic	oxygen
derogative	metropolitan	phenomenon
despondent	misogynist	philosophy
dialogue	mnemonic (*first* m *silent*)	policy
document	moderate	popular
dominant	modicum	positive
ecology	modify	posterity
economy	modulate	poverty
elongate	molecule	predominant
emollient	monastery	predominate
esophagus	monitor	preponderance
evocative	monologue	prerogative
geography	monopoly	probable

►

prodigy

prognostic

prognosticate

propagate

prosecute

solitary

soluble

sovereign

symbolic

synopsis

theology

thermometer

velocity

volunteer

OŎ IN ONE-SYLLABLE WORDS

co- (*prefix*)	cone	grove
bloat	cope	grow
blow	cove	hoax
boast	croak	hoe
boat	crow	hold
bold	doe	hole
bolt	dome	holt
bone	don't	home
both	dose	hone
bow	dote	hope
bowl	dough (*final gh silent*)	hose
broach	doze	host
broke	droll	joke
choke	drone	jolt
chose	drove	knoll
chrome	float	know
cloak	flow	load
close	foam	loaf
clothe	foe	loan
clothes	fold	low
clove	folk (*l is silent*)	moan
coach	froze	mode
coal	ghost	mold
coast	gloat	mole
coat	globe	mope
coax	glow	most
code	go	mow
coke	goal	no
cold	goat	node
cole	gold	nose
colt	grope	note
comb	gross	oak

OŎ IN ONE-SYLLABLE WORDS (CONTINUED)

◄
oath	rode	stroll
oh	role	those
old	roll	though*
owe	rope	throat
own	rose	throne
phone	row	throw
poach	scold	toast
poke	scope	toe
pole	scroll	told
poll	show	tone
pose	slow	vogue
post	smoke	vote
pro	snow	whole
probe	so	woke
prone	sold	won't
prose	sole	wove
quote	soul	wrote
road	stole	yolk (l *is silent*)
roam	stone	zone
roast	stove	
robe	stroke	

OŎ IN TWO-SYLLABLE WORDS

abode	approach	bestow
afloat	arose	billow
ago	arrow	bingo
alcove	astro	bogus
almost	atone	bolder
alone	auto	bolster
also	awoke	bonus
although*	behold	brochure
alto	bellow	bureau†
Anglo	below	burrow

►

---

*The *gh* in these words is silent and not pronounced.

†This is an exception to the spelling patterns of oŏ.

◄ cajole

callow

cargo

charcoal

chemo

clover

cobra

cocoa

colon

coma

compose

connote

console

control

cozy

cyclone

demote

denote

devote

dispose

donate

donor

ego

elbow

elope

enclose

engross

ergo

evoke

explode

expose

fellow

focus

glucose

gopher

hello

hero

holster

holy

hormone

hotel

impose

intone

invoke

local

locust

lotion

lotus

mango

marrow

mellow

microbe

mobile

molten

moment

motion

motive

motor

narrow

noble

nomad

notice

notion

obese

obey

oboe

ocean

odor

ogle

omen

omit

only

opal

opaque

open

oppose

oval

over

overt

ozone

parole

patrol

phoneme

photo

pillow

poem

polar

pony

potion

poultry

presto

proceeds (*noun*)

proclaim

procure

profile

program

promote

propose

protein

protest (*noun*)

provoke

pseudo

psycho

quota

remote

repose

reproach

revoke

revolt

rotate

shadow

slogan

social

sofa

solar

solo

suppose ►

OŬ IN TWO-SYLLABLE WORDS (*CONTINUED*)

◄

swollen	trophy	window
thorough*	vocal	yellow
total	widow	yoga
trio	willow	zero

OŬ IN WORDS OF THREE OR MORE SYLLABLES

-mony (*suffix*)	casino	foliage
acidosis	casserole	hypnosis
acrimony	ceremony	isotope
adobe	chaperone	juxtapose
aerobic	chromosome	location
alimony	coconut	locomotion
ambrosia	cohabit	magnolia
amino	coherence	matrimony
anaerobic	cohesion	mediocre
anecdote	coincide	metronome
antelope	coincidence	microphone
antidote	colloquial	microscope
appropriate	component	misnomer
archipelago	composure	negotiate
aroma	condolence	neurosis
artichoke	copious	November
associate	cornucopia	oasis
association	corrosion	opponent
atrocious	coyote	patio
audio	diagnose	patrimony
baloney	diploma	persona
baritone	embargo	phobia
begonia	embryo	phonograph
binomial	envelope	photograph
biochemistry	episode	piano
buffalo	erosion	placebo
bungalow	exponent	pneumonia
cameo	ferocious	podium
cantaloupe	fiasco	portfolio

►

---

*The *gh* in this word is silent and not pronounced.

◄

potato	proponent	stereo
precocious	proscenium	studio
probation	radio	vociferous
procrastinate	ratio	zodiac

a FOLLOWED BY *oŏ* IN THE SAME TWO-SYLLABLE WORD

borrow	follow	nachos
bravo	hollow	sorrow
compost	macho	swallow
condo	motto	trombone

oŏ FOLLOWED BY *a* IN THE SAME TWO-SYLLABLE WORD

co-op	proton
prologue	robot
prolong	

a FOLLOWED BY *oŏ* IN THE SAME WORD OF THREE OR MORE SYLLABLES

avocado	October	scenario
bravado	osmosis	soprano
comatose	pistachio	tomorrow
monotone	prognosis	volcano

oŏ FOLLOWED BY *a* IN THE SAME WORD OF THREE OR MORE SYLLABLES

| koala |
| protocol |

Sentences: *a*

CD
40

Turn to **CD Track 40.** Listen to the recording of the following sentences, then read the sentences aloud. Concentrate on correctly pronouncing the *a* sound, which is marked phonetically.

           a   a   a
1 Who should we contact about the monumental anthology?

       a   a   a   a
2 I was astonished when my colleague dodged the conflict.

3 Do astronomy and astrology have anything in common, or are they
at odds?

4 During the conference, John's boss acknowledged the unsolved problem.

5 Robert made a colossal mistake when he dissolved the contract.

6 You should apologize for your chronically negative comments.

7 The choreographer's novel work showed confidence and promise.

8 Colleen's optimism was challenged when she lost the contest.

9 There are often consequences to compromising on a project.

10 Conrad's doctor offered a positive prognosis.

11 Her response prompted me to adopt a stricter policy.

12 The song is nostalgic and evocative of Hollywood drama.

13 I'm bothered by the car horn's constant, long honking.

14 Is it logical to copy pompous mediocrity?

15 It can feel horrible when job hunting in a bad economy.

Sentences: oŭ

Turn to CD Track 41. Listen to the recording of the following sentences, then read the sentences aloud. Concentrate on correctly pronouncing the oŭ sound, which is marked phonetically.

1 Do you expect Joseph to close the auto deal alone?

2 The aroma from the sole casserole arose from the stove.

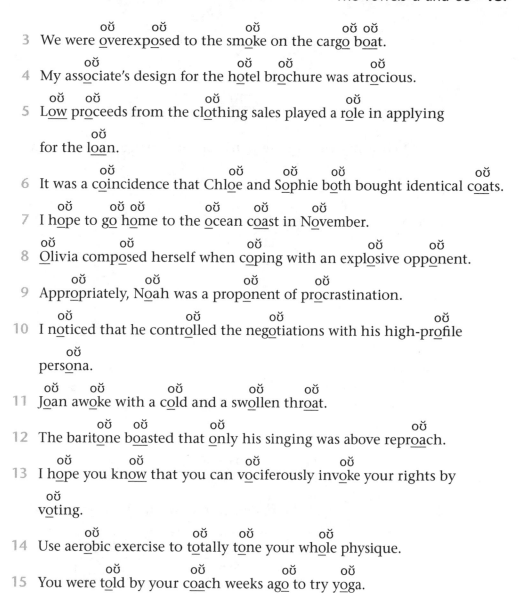

$\quad\quad\quad$ o˘o $\quad\quad$ o˘o $\quad\quad\quad\quad$ o˘o $\quad\quad\quad\quad$ o˘o o˘o
3 We were <u>o</u>verexp<u>o</u>sed to the sm<u>o</u>ke on the carg<u>o</u> b<u>oa</u>t.

$\quad\quad\quad$ o˘o $\quad\quad\quad\quad\quad$ o˘o o˘o $\quad\quad\quad$ o˘o
4 My ass<u>o</u>ciate's design for the h<u>o</u>tel br<u>o</u>chure was atr<u>o</u>cious.

$\quad\quad$ o˘o o˘o $\quad\quad\quad\quad$ o˘o $\quad\quad\quad\quad$ o˘o
5 L<u>ow</u> pr<u>o</u>ceeds from the cl<u>o</u>thing sales played a r<u>o</u>le in applying

$\quad\quad\quad$ o˘o
for the l<u>oa</u>n.

$\quad\quad\quad$ o˘o $\quad\quad\quad\quad$ o˘o $\quad$ o˘o $\quad$ o˘o $\quad\quad\quad\quad$ o˘o
6 It was a c<u>o</u>incidence that Chl<u>o</u>e and S<u>o</u>phie b<u>o</u>th bought identical c<u>oa</u>ts.

$\quad\quad$ o˘o $\quad\quad$ o˘o o˘o $\quad\quad$ o˘o $\quad\quad$ o˘o $\quad\quad$ o˘o
7 I h<u>o</u>pe to g<u>o</u> h<u>o</u>me to the <u>o</u>cean c<u>oa</u>st in N<u>o</u>vember.

o˘o $\quad\quad\quad$ o˘o $\quad\quad\quad\quad$ o˘o $\quad\quad\quad\quad$ o˘o $\quad$ o˘o
8 <u>O</u>livia comp<u>o</u>sed herself when c<u>o</u>ping with an expl<u>o</u>sive opp<u>o</u>nent.

$\quad\quad$ o˘o $\quad\quad\quad$ o˘o $\quad\quad\quad$ o˘o $\quad\quad$ o˘o
9 Appropriately, N<u>o</u>ah was a prop<u>o</u>nent of pr<u>o</u>crastination.

$\quad\quad$ o˘o $\quad\quad\quad\quad$ o˘o $\quad\quad$ o˘o $\quad\quad\quad\quad\quad$ o˘o
10 I n<u>o</u>ticed that he contr<u>o</u>lled the neg<u>o</u>tiations with his high-pr<u>o</u>file

$\quad$ o˘o
pers<u>o</u>na.

$\quad$ o˘o $\quad$ o˘o $\quad\quad\quad$ o˘o $\quad\quad$ o˘o $\quad$ o˘o
11 J<u>oa</u>n aw<u>o</u>ke with a c<u>o</u>ld and a sw<u>o</u>llen thr<u>oa</u>t.

$\quad\quad\quad$ o˘o o˘o $\quad\quad\quad$ o˘o $\quad\quad\quad\quad\quad\quad$ o˘o
12 The barit<u>o</u>ne b<u>oa</u>sted that <u>o</u>nly his singing was above repr<u>oa</u>ch.

$\quad\quad$ o˘o $\quad\quad\quad$ o˘o $\quad\quad\quad\quad$ o˘o $\quad\quad$ o˘o
13 I h<u>o</u>pe you kn<u>ow</u> that you can v<u>o</u>ciferously inv<u>o</u>ke your rights by

$\quad$ o˘o
v<u>o</u>ting.

$\quad\quad$ o˘o $\quad\quad\quad$ o˘o $\quad$ o˘o $\quad\quad$ o˘o
14 Use aer<u>o</u>bic exercise to t<u>o</u>tally t<u>o</u>ne your wh<u>o</u>le physique.

$\quad\quad\quad$ o˘o $\quad\quad\quad$ o˘o $\quad\quad$ o˘o $\quad$ o˘o
15 You were t<u>o</u>ld by your c<u>oa</u>ch weeks ag<u>o</u> to try y<u>o</u>ga.

Sentences: *a* vs. *o˘o*

CD

42

*Turn to **CD Track 42**.* Listen to the recording of the following sentences, then read the sentences aloud. Concentrate on distinguishing between the *a* and *o˘o* sounds, which are marked phonetically.

1 Can we borrow a copy of the consolidated notes?

2 Follow your heart and soul—you won't be sorry!

3 Let's contemplate the pros and cons of every option.

4 Out of curiosity, will your response of "no" change by tomorrow?

5 Joe and John were obviously bothered about leaving home.

6 Prolong your holiday, but don't overdo the shopping.

7 Ironically, it's almost as though Bob wanted to complicate the scenario.

8 The phenomenon of strong comedy often results after dramatic moments.

9 She focused on the probability of growing her own portfolio in commodity trading.

10 Colleen played the oboe, the trombone, and the piano.

11 The precocious, bold photographer imposed his style on the project.

12 Is the volunteer responsible for monitoring old protocol?

13 Can your body cross beyond limitations and prolong yoga poses?

14 Correspond via the phone so as not to complicate contradictory conversations.

15 Let's hope posterity will prosper from our resolve to modify soil erosion.

PART THREE

THE RHYTHMS OF ENGLISH

SEVENTEEN

Syllable stress within words

When we think of "stress," we normally associate it with such feelings as discomfort, agitation, and even duress. You may have experienced these feelings in the course of studying English. But "stress" in this and the following chapter denotes far more than these emotional reactions. The principle of stress in spoken English dictates its innate rhythm and intonation.

There are two main areas in which we employ stress: (1) syllable stress within words and (2) word emphasis within sentences. We'll explore sentence stress in Chapter Eighteen. Right now, let's consider stress within words.

All words containing two or more syllables give main emphasis to one primary syllable. This is accomplished by making that syllable longer, louder, and higher in pitch. Say the following words aloud, and notice how the stressed syllable within each is emphasized.

> trad**í**tion
> anniv**é**rsary
> **né**cessary
> **bréa**kable
> **mír**ror
> engin**cér**

If you have trouble hearing where the stress within a word lies, try the following exercise, using the word *tradition*. *Tradition* has three distinct syllables. Try saying it three different ways: ***trá**dition, tra**dí**tion, tradi**tión***. Each time you say the boldfaced syllable, stamp your foot on that syllable.

This will automatically cause you to pronounce that syllable longer, louder, and higher in pitch. By shifting the stress in this way, you will be able to recognize where the syllable stress falls within a word. In our example, the syllable stress falls on the second syllable: *tradítion*.

Often, stress within words isn't predictable and can seem arbitrary, since English has incorporated vocabulary from so many other languages. There are, however, a few rules that we can use to predict syllable stress.

Noun and verb variants

One rule—which applies to words that can be either a noun or a verb—is that two-syllable nouns are usually stressed on the first syllable, and two-syllable verbs are stressed on the second syllable. Consider the following examples.

NOUNS	VERBS
cómpound	to compóund
cóntrast	to contrást
cóntest	to contést
ímport	to impórt
ínsert	to insért
cóntract	to contráct
pérmit	to permít
tránsport	to transpórt

A second rule is that a compound noun (two nouns blended together to form a new word) has its stress on the first noun, as in the following examples.

COMPOUND NOUNS
báll·park
néws·paper
fíre·man
boók·case
staír·well

►

◄   wáter·fall
       seá·side
       wáll·paper

By contrast, in a phrasal verb (a verb coupled with a preposition or adverb), the second element is stressed, as in the following examples.

PHRASAL VERBS

to get **úp**
to go **óut**
to break **ín**
to stand **óut**
to wake **úp**
to let **gó**
to make **úp**
to give **ín**

The principle of vowel reduction

Adding to the confusion of the correspondence between spelling patterns and pronunciation in English is the principle of vowel reduction. Every word in English carries primary stress on one of its syllables. Most of the vowels in the unstressed syllables are reduced to a schwa, which is phonetically represented by ə. This is a neutral sound, similar to the phoneme in the word *uh*. Thus, the words *loyal, introduction,* and *commandment* are pronounced ˈlɔĭəl, ɪntrəˈdʌkʃən, and kəˈmændmənt. Vowel reduction makes it imperative that you find the correctly stressed syllable in a word, since many of the vowels in the unstressed syllables are reduced, changing the pronunciation of their phonemes altogether.

Two common spelling patterns that can take either the strong vowel ɑ or the weak vowel ə, depending on where the primary syllable stress lies in a word, are *com-* and *con-*; compare *comment* (ˈkɑment) and *commit* (kəˈmɪt). Following is a list of common English words with these spelling patterns. In all of these words, the vowel in the *com-* and *con-* spelling pattern is in a prefix or unstressed position and is pronounced ə.

com-

combatant	communal	complain
combine (*verb*)	communicate	complaint
combustible	communion	complaisance
combustion	community	complete
comedian/comedienne	commute	complexion
command	commuter	compliance
commander	companion	comply
commandment	comparative	component
commemorate	compare	compose
commence	compartment	composite
commencement	compassion	composure
commercial	compatible	compress (*verb*)
commiserate	compel	comprise
commission	compete	compulsive
commit	competitive	compunction
commitment	competitor	compute
committee	compile	computer
commotion	complacent	

con-

conceal	concussion	conform
concede	condemn	confront
conceited	condense	confuse
conceive	conditioner	congeal
concentric	condolence	congenial
conception	condone	congested
concern	conduct (*verb*)	conglomerate
concerted	confection	congressional
concerto	confederacy	conjecture
concession	confer	conjunction
conciliatory	confess	connect
concise	confetti	consecutive
conclusion	confide	consent
concoct	configuration	conservative
concomitant	confine	conserve
concordance	confirm	consider
concur	conflicted	considerate ►

◄ consignment   contagious   contrite

consistency   contain   contrive

consistent   contaminate   control

console   contempt   contusion

consolidate   contend   conundrum

consort (*verb*)   content (*adjective*)   convene

conspicuous   contest (*verb*)   convenient

conspire   contingency   convention

constituency   continual   converge

constrain   continue   convert (*verb*)

constrict   continuum   convertible

construct (*verb*)   contortion   convey

construe   contraction   convict (*verb*)

consult (*verb*)   contralto   convince

consume   contraption   convulsion

consumption   contribute

Suffix spelling patterns that affect syllable stress

Most suffixes fall into three groups: (1) those from Old English and other Germanic languages, (2) those from Latin through Old French, and (3) those from Greek.

The suffixes derived from Old English (such as *-ness, -en, -ish, -like,* and *-ern*) do not influence syllable stress. However, we can isolate 21 Latin and Greek suffixes that, when added to the roots of words, usually shift the stress (but, of course, there are always exceptions in English). Additionally, 10 suffixes derived from Old French receive primary stress themselves.

The following Latin and Greek suffixes shift the stress within words to the syllable right before the suffix.

SUFFIX	WORD	WORD WITH SUFFIX
-tion	**áu**thorize	authorizátion
-sion	**pér**mit	permíssion
-ic	**hé**ro	heróic
-tic	**fán**tasy	fantástic

►

SUFFIX	WORD	WORD WITH SUFFIX
-ical	**hí**story	his**tó**rical
-ial	**é**ditor	edi**tó**rial
-ian	**mú**sic	mu**sí**cian
-ity	e**léc**tric	elec**trí**city
-ety	**só**cial	so**cí**ety
-ify	**hú**mid	hu**mí**dify
-graphy	**phó**to	pho**tó**graphy
-logy	**phý**sics	physi**ó**logy
-cracy	**bú**reau	bu**reáu**cracy
-ual	**ín**tellect	intel**léc**tual
-ious	**ín**dustry	in**dús**trious
-eous	**ér**ror	er**ró**neous

The following Latin and Greek suffixes dictate that the stress within words falls two syllables before the suffix.

SUFFIX	WORD	WORD WITH SUFFIX
-graph	pho**tó**graphy	**phó**tograph
-crat	de**mó**cracy	**dé**mocrat
-ate	de**món**strative	**dé**monstrate
-ar	**réc**tangle	rec**tán**gular
-ize	im**mú**ne	**ím**munize

The following suffixes are derived from Old French, and they receive primary stress themselves.

SUFFIX	WORD
-ade	lemon**áde**
-eur/-euse	mas**seúr**/mas**seúse**
-air/-aire	debo**náir**
-eer	pio**neér**
-ette	usher**étte**
-ese	Japan**ése**
-esque	pictur**ésque**
-ee	refer**eé**
-ique	tech**níque**
-oon	bal**loón**

Examples

Following are lists of common English words with Latin and Greek suffixes that shift the stress within words to the syllable right before the suffix.

-tion	*-sion*
administrátion	commíssion
associátion	compássion
communicátion	conclúsion
cooperátion	confúsion
exclamátion	discússion
explanátion	expréssion
identificátion	impréssion
organizátion	posséssion
recognítion	procéssion
transportátion	proféssion

-ic	*-tic*
acadèmic	artístic
diabólic	automátic
económic	characterístic
eléctric	enthusiástic
electrónic	magnétic
geográphic*	democrátic*
horrífic	statístic
mechánic	sympathétic
orgánic	romántic
scientífic	dramátic

---

*If a word contains two or more suffixes that affect stress, the last suffix determines the stress within the word.

-ical	-ial
biológical*	binómial†
económical	colónial†
ecuménical	commércial
idéntical	esséntial
mathemátical	indústrial†
músical	matérial†
physiológical*	offícial
polítical	presidéntial
theorétical	residéntial
týpical	substántial

-ian	-ity
beautícian	abílity
custódian‡	capácity
guárdian‡	continúity
histórian‡	finálity
magícian	minórity
obstetrícian	nationálity
physícian	possibílity
polítician	probabílity
technícian	sensitívity
utópian‡	univérsity

---

*If a word contains two or more suffixes that affect stress, the last suffix determines the stress within the word.

†The -ial suffix of these words is pronounced as two syllables: iəl. For the other words in the list, the suffix is pronounced as one syllable: əl.

‡The -ian suffix of these words is pronounced as two syllables: iən. For the other words in the list, the suffix is pronounced as one syllable: ən.

-ety	*-ify*
anx**í**ety	a**cí**dify
im**pí**ety	**clás**sify
impro**prí**ety	**có**dify
moíety	di**vér**sify
na**í**vety	e**múl**sify
noto**rí**ety	i**dén**tify
pro**prí**ety	**mó**dify
so**brí**ety	ob**jéc**tify
so**cí**ety	**quá**lify
va**rí**ety	so**lí**dify

-graphy	*-logy*
bibli**ó**graphy	anesthesi**ó**logy
bi**ó**graphy	an**thó**logy
cal**lí**graphy	anthro**pó**logy
car**tó**graphy	archae**ó**logy
chore**ó**graphy	as**tró**logy
cinema**tó**graphy	bi**ó**logy
ge**ó**graphy	cardi**ó**logy
li**thó**graphy	e**có**logy
ste**nó**graphy	ge**ó**logy
to**pó**graphy	pa**thó**logy

-cracy	*-ual*
aris**tó**cracy	ac**cén**tual
au**tó**cracy	con**cép**tual
bu**reáu**cracy	con**téx**tual
de**mó**cracy	con**trác**tual
hie**ró**cracy	ha**bí**tual
mo**nó**cracy	indi**ví**dual
physi**ó**cracy	ins**tínc**tual
plu**tó**cracy	intel**léc**tual
tech**nó**cracy	per**pé**tual
the**ó**cracy	re**sí**dual

-ious	*-eous*
delírious	advantágeous*
harmónious	**beáuteous**
labórious	courágeous*
luxúrious	extemporáneous
melódious	extráneous
mystérious	instantáneous
suspícious*	miscelláneous
tédious	outrágeous*
várious	simultáneous
victórious	spontáneous

Following are lists of common English words with Latin and Greek suffixes that dictate that the stress within words falls two syllables before the suffix.

-graph	*-crat*
áutograph	arístocrat
épigraph	**áu**tocrat
hólograph	**bú**reaucrat
líthograph	**dé**mocrat
páragraph	**plú**tocrat
pólygraph	**téch**nocrat
télegraph	**thé**ocrat

---

*In these words, the suffixes *-ious* and *-eous* are pronounced as one syllable: əs. For the other words in the lists, the suffix is pronounced as two syllables: iəs.

*-ate**	*-ar*
áccurate	alvé**olar**
ádequate	**án**gular
cóncentrate	avún**cular**
démonstrate	cardiovás**cular**
éducate	extracurrí**cular**
el**á**borate	molé**cular**
éstimate	partí**cular**
índicate	perpendí**cular**
intermé**diate**	**ré**gular
óperate	spectá**cular**

-ize
acc**és**sorize
an**és**thetize
attit**ú**dinize
áuthorize
bu**reáu**cratize
críticize
depart**mén**talize
émphasize
eúlogize
in**í**tialize

---

*The suffix *-ate* is pronounced ɪt if the word is a noun or adjective, and eɪt if the word is a verb.

Following are lists of common English words with suffixes derived from Old French; the suffixes themselves have primary stress.

-ade	*-eur/-euse**
arcáde	chantéuse
blockáde	chaufféur
brigáde	connoisséur
crusáde	entreprenéur
dissuáde	liquéur
grenáde	masséuse
masqueráde	restauratéur
persuáde	sabotéur
stockáde	voyéur

-air(e)	*-eer*
au páir	auctionéer
au contráire	caréer
billionáire	commandéer
concessionáire	enginéer
doctrináire	musketéer
legionnáire	puppetéer
millionáire	racketéer
questionnáire	voluntéer

-ette	*-ese*
bachelorétte	Chinése
brunétte	legalése
cassétte	Maltése
majorétte	obése
roulétte	Pekingése
silhouétte	Siamése
vinaigrétte	Viennése

---

*The French suffix *-euse* denotes the feminine form of masculine nouns ending in *-eur*.

-esque	*-ee*
arabésque	addresseé
burlésque	adviseé
chivalrésque	chimpanzeé
grotésque	devoteé
picturésque	divorceé
Romanésque	guaranteé
statuésque	jamboreé

-ique	*-oon*
antíque	baboón
boutíque	buffoón
critíque	cartoón
mystíque	harpoón
oblíque	macaroón
physíque	raccoón
uníque	saloón

Sentences

CD
43

*Turn to **CD Track 43**.* Listen to the recording of the following sentences, then read the sentences aloud. Concentrate on the syllable stress within individual words as dictated by suffix spelling patterns.

1 Jennifer's abílity to reach a polítical conclúsion solídified her posítion as a cándidate.

2 Clarificátion of the económic ideólogy produced satisfáction among the Démocrats.

3 The mystíque of the eláborate concéptual choreógraphy caused anxíety in the dancers.

4 The económical decísions of Andrew's guárdian were aúthorized by law.

5 The auctioneér took bids on aútographs of aristócracy from histórical periods.

6 Stephen was an entrepre**neúr**; no wonder he became such a successful restaura**teúr**.

7 Playing with my Peking**ése** puppy, Wally, guaran**teéd** hours of perp**ét**ual delight.

8 The enthusi**ás**tic toddler was **cón**centrated on the va**rí**ety of brightly colored bal**loóns**.

9 Pam spoke extempo**rá**neously about **ém**phasizing the positive during cri**tíques**.

10 Do all elec**trón**ic devices require techno**lóg**ical skill to **mín**imize frus**trá**tion?

EIGHTEEN

Word stress within sentences

The rhythm of English speech

Native speakers of English know which words to emphasize and which to "throw away," and therefore have little trouble figuring out how to make even the most complex of sentences fluent. Nonnative speakers of English have a far more arduous task: An English sentence often contains many small words that do not carry the essential meaning of the idea or thought. A common mistake made by nonnative speakers is to pronounce every word with equal stress, creating a very stilted rhythm that does not match that of native English speakers.

To understand the rhythm of English speech, it is useful to differentiate between operative and inoperative words.

Operative words

Operative words carry the meaning of a sentence and therefore conjure an image in the listener's mind. There are four categories of these words.

Verbs
Nouns
Adjectives
Adverbs

Inoperative words

Inoperative words are largely responsible for the syntax, or structure, of sentences; they don't carry the key meaning of the thought being communicated and are therefore "thrown away"—that is, pronounced with very little emphasis. In some of these words, the vowel can be reduced to the weak form of the schwa ə. There are several categories of these words.

Articles
Prepositions
Conjunctions
Pronouns (Although they are often the subject of a sentence,
    pronouns refer to a noun mentioned earlier in the discourse.)
Auxiliary verbs
The verb *to be* in all its forms
The first word of infinitives, as in *to look* (The word *to* is reduced
    to the weak form.)

Of course, rhythm is ultimately the choice of the speaker. But as a general guideline, distinguishing between operative and inoperative words allows a nonnative speaker to more accurately create the natural rhythm of English speech. And if one reduces the stress of all inoperative words while giving more stress to the operative words, the thought or meaning of the communication will be much clearer.

Weak forms

Certain words in English can have two distinct pronunciations: a strong form and a weak form. Always use the weak forms of these words unless the strong form is needed to change the meaning of the sentence.

ARTICLES

WEAK FORM	STRONG FORM
ə a	eĭ a
ə an	æ an
ə the*	i the

PREPOSITIONS

WEAK FORM	STRONG FORM
ə at	æ at
ɚ for	ɔɚ for
ə from	ʌ from
ə of	ʌ of
ə to	u to
ə into	u into

CONJUNCTIONS

WEAK FORM	STRONG FORM
ə and	æ and
ə but	ʌ but
ə than	æ than
ɚ or	ɔɚ or
ɚ nor	ɔɚ nor

PRONOUNS

WEAK FORM	STRONG FORM
ɚ her	ɝ her
ə them	e them
ə us	ʌ us
ɚ your	ʊɚ your
ə some	ʌ some
ə that	æ that

*However, always use ði when the next word begins with a vowel.

AUXILIARY VERBS

WEAK FORM	STRONG FORM	WEAK FORM	STRONG FORM
ə am	æ am	ə has	æ has
ɚ are	ɑɚ are	ə have	æ have
ə can	æ can	ə must	ʌ must
ə could	ʊ could	ə shall	æ shall
ə do	u do	ə should	ʊ should
ə does	ʌ does	ə was	ʌ was
ə had	æ had	ɚ were	ɝ were

Examples of strong forms vs. weak forms

from

Where are you fr**ʌ**om?

Bob is fr**ə**om Denver.

of

When you're under stress, what do you think **ʌ**of?

Meg dreams **ə**of the sea.

for

Who is the gift f**ɔɚ**or?

I bought that f**ɚ**or Anne.

but

No "b$\underset{\wedge}{u}$t"s about it!

I want to swim, b$\underset{\ni}{u}$t it's too cold.

some

I don't want all of the pudding, but I want s$\hat{o}$me.

Mike ate s$\overset{\ni}{o}$me fruit.

are

I'm not going out, but they <u>$\overset{ɑɚ}{are}$</u>.

$\overset{ɚ}{\underline{Are}}$ you sure you're finished?

has

I want what he h$\overset{æ}{a}$s!

He h$\overset{\ni}{a}$s a quick wit.

does

Yes, she d$\overset{\wedge}{oe}$s!

D$\overset{\ni}{oe}$s Mary have a cat?

was

Tom w$\overset{\ni}{a}$sn't happy, but Ed w$\hat{a}$s.

I w$\overset{\ni}{a}$s about to volunteer.

them

I met with Neil, but not with th<u>e</u>m.

We could invite th<u>e</u>m to the party.

Contrasting operative and inoperative words

Following is an exercise in practicing the natural rhythms of English speech. Follow the steps below.

1. Underline all the operative words in a sentence.
2. Cross out all the inoperative words in a sentence.
3. Now, read aloud only the underlined operative words. Notice that they make sense and convey the essential meaning of the sentence without the inoperative words.
4. Finally, read the entire sentence aloud. Notice if this affects the rhythm to which you are normally accustomed.

Just as primary stress within words makes a *syllable* longer, louder, and higher in pitch, so stressing operative words in sentences makes those *words* longer, louder, and higher in pitch. Reading aloud enables you to listen and correct yourself as you work toward a more natural rhythm and flow of English speech.

Sentences

In the following sentences, the operative words are underlined and the inoperative words are crossed out. The weak forms of words are marked with the schwa ə phoneme. Following the steps above, read aloud only the operative words in a sentence, and notice that the thought still makes sense. Then read the entire sentence aloud, giving the inoperative words less stress than the operative words. You will notice an improvement in your intonation. You can check yourself by listening to a recording of these sentences on *CD Track 44.*

CD
44

           ə   ə   ə ə

1 Kate ~~would have~~ loved ~~to have~~ gone ~~on~~ vacation.

              ə   ə   ə   ə

2 ~~Is it a~~ crime ~~to~~ witness ~~a~~ robbery ~~and~~ say nothing?

         ə   ə   ə ə

3 Pam ~~is a~~ valued colleague ~~as~~ well ~~as the~~ perfect boss.

                ɚ   ɚ

4 Cheesecake ~~for~~ breakfast—~~are you~~ kidding ~~me~~?

                 ə   ə   ə

5 Study hard ~~and~~ practice frequently, ~~and you will be~~ sure ~~to~~ see results.

        ə   ə   ə

6 ~~Can you~~ believe ~~that~~ another year ~~has~~ gone by so quickly?

                            ə   ə

7 ~~If~~ raised together, puppies ~~and~~ kittens ~~can be~~ terrific playmates.

         ə   ə ə   ə   ə ə   ə

8 ~~The~~ first half ~~of the~~ movie ~~was~~ great, ~~but the~~ second half ~~was~~ disappointing.

                    ə   ə ɚ

9 ~~Did you~~ think ~~the~~ fashion show contained clothing lines ~~that were~~ extreme?

           ə   ə   ə

10 ~~After a~~ long day's work, ~~I~~ enjoy ~~the~~ company ~~of my~~ friends.

Speaking in phrases and clauses

    The last piece in the puzzle of English intonation is to speak in phrases and clauses. A **phrase** is a group of words that may contain nouns and verbs, but it does not have a subject acting on a verb. A **clause** is a group of words that contains a subject that is acting on a verb. Independent clauses can stand on their own as sentences; dependent clauses cannot stand on their own and are secondary thoughts within sentences.

    This sounds technical, but the rhythm of English speech is achieved by grouping patterns of words around a central idea. Just as we cautioned against breaking a sentence into individual words, we must also warn against trying to deal with the entire sentence at once. Depending on your past training, you may have been taught to impose an overall sing-song rhythm on English, and indeed, to nonnative speakers, English speech may sound melodious, rhythmic, and fairly arbitrary. But English intonation is actually quite specific: You must distill sentences into phrases and clauses in order to use operative and inoperative words effectively.

The essential communication of a phrase or clause is the expression of an image. In its purest form, the thought of a speaker is condensed into an image or picture that is readily grasped by the listener. This sounds complicated, but is relatively intuitive. Consider the following phrases.

> a long day's work
> a frisky puppy playing
> an abandoned red barn

Each of these phrases probably conjures a definite image in your mind, which will in turn translate into a very specific picture in the minds of your listeners. Consider the following sentence.

> After a long day's work, I was reinvigorated by the sight
> of a frisky puppy playing in an abandoned red barn.

Now, let's bracket these phrases within the sentence.

> [After a long day's work], [I was reinvigorated] by [the sight
> of a frisky puppy playing] in [an abandoned red barn].

Notice how much more specific your intonation is by breaking the sentence into phrases, or basic units of thoughts. We can analyze this sentence further by marking the operative and inoperative words, as follows.

> [~~After a~~ long day's work], [~~I was~~ reinvigorated] ~~by~~ [~~the~~ sight
> ~~of a~~ frisky puppy playing] ~~in~~ [~~an~~ abandoned red barn].

Intonation or pitch variance

Many nonnative speakers have been taught that English uses "staircase intonation"—that a speaker should inflect as if lightly bounding down a flight of stairs toward the period at the end of the sentence. But operative words are longer, louder, and higher in pitch, and as you can see in the example above, they generally fall toward the end of phrases and clauses. While native English speakers do inflect downward at the ends of sentences, *the downward inflection occurs only on the final phoneme of the sentence.* If we were to score the pitch in the sentence above, it would look like the following.

                    long day's work],   reinvigorated]   sight
[After a ─────────────────── [I was ─────────────── by [the ──────
              frisky puppy playing]   abandoned red ba
of a ─────────────────────── in [an ───────────────────rn].

It is only the final phoneme that inflects downward, making the statement a declarative sentence. (In this case, it is the r coloring attached to the consonant n.) Similarly, *it is the upward inflection of the final phoneme that turns a statement into a question.* If we were to score the pitch of the interrogative sentence *Would you like some coffee?* it would look like the following.

                                      fee?
                    like   cof ────
Would you ──── some ────

In the sample paragraphs below, the operative words are underlined and the inoperative words are crossed out. The images, or phrases, are bracketed. Read the paragraphs aloud. Notice that the operative words are longer, louder, and higher in pitch than the inoperative words. Remember to inflect downward on the final phoneme of declarative sentences, and to inflect upward on the final phoneme of interrogative sentences.

*The following paragraph is recorded on **CD Track 45**.*

CD
45

Meg and Ed

[Meg and Ed] were [fond of the countryside]. They [loved the fresh air], the [lush foliage], and the [smells and sounds of the outdoors]. However, they were [not fond of exercise], and therefore did [not enjoy hiking]. [One sunny afternoon], they [decided to take a drive through the country]. They [saw a sign advertising fresh produce] and [decided to pull over] and [buy vegetables for dinner]. They [got out of the car] and [went into the small store]. [Ten minutes later], [Meg and Ed emerged with cucumbers, tomatoes, peaches, and pears]. But [when they reached their car], they [discovered one of their tires was flat]. The [nearest gas station] was a [mile away]. Not only did [Meg and Ed purchase delicious produce], they were also [forced to take a hike in the country].

CD

46

*The following paragraph is recorded on **CD Track 46**.*

Rhonda's vacation

[Rhonda] was [fond of all water sports]. She [enjoyed waterskiing, surfing, and sailing]. But [most of all, she loved to snorkel]. On [one vacation in the Caribbean], she [joined an adventurous tour group] that [rented kayaks] and [paddled across] to a [small deserted island a mile away]. She [put on her mask and flippers] and [dove under the pale blue water]. [Rhonda was astonished] at the [wide variety of fish] and at the [beautiful array of colors surrounding] her, so she [swam out farther] to [continue exploring]. She was [even more astonished an hour later], when she [swam back in] and [found her group had left without her]. [Rhonda began to panic]. Her [heart started to race]. Was she [left alone on a deserted island]!? Suddenly, [another group of kayaks] [came around the bend of the cove], and [Rhonda remembered] that there was a [new tour group] that [set off from the hotel every hour].

The same method of scoring can be used for business presentations. Let's turn now to the final chapter of *Perfecting Your English Pronunciation,* and learn how to mark a business speech.

PART FOUR

PUTTING IT ALL TOGETHER

NINETEEN

Marking a business speech

How to prepare for a presentation

Let's take all the lessons from this book and apply them in an organized fashion in order to drastically improve your performance when giving presentations in English.

If you have worked through this book chapter by chapter, you know what your problem sounds are and how to correct them. You also have an understanding of operative and inoperative words and of speaking in phrases and clauses to allow your listeners to better image the content of your communication. To prepare for your presentation, print out a copy of it (double spaced, so you have space for your marks) and grab a pencil. Let's get started.

Step 1: Marking difficult sounds

Begin by marking all of your difficult sounds. Put the phonetic symbols for these challenging sounds directly above their English spelling equivalents. Following are three examples of Fred's business pitches, with problem sounds marked phonetically.

Fred's business pitch No. 1
(marked for the sounds ð/θ, r, ɪ, and oŭ/ɑ)

  ð   ɑ oŭ ɪ   r   ɑ   r
The following PowerPoint presentation on your computer screen

oŭ ɪ r ɪ   ɪ r   oŭoŭ   r oŭ
focuses on creating a different portfolio scenario for your client's

ɪ ɪ   ɪ ɪ ɪ   ɪ   ɪ   ɑ ɪ   r   ɑ
dividends. It is examined using an economic deceleration model,

      ɪ ɪ   ɪ ɑ ð   ɪ   r   ɪ   ɪ
as delineated on the accompanying spreadsheets. In our opinion,

                 ɑ   ɪ ɪ   ɪ   ɪ   ɪ   ɪ r
your client's company stock dividends will be impacted and increase

r   ɪ   ɪ ð ɪ   oŭoŭ r   ɪ ɪ   ɪ ɪ ð
dramatically if this portfolio structure is implemented in the next

 ɪ   θ   ɪ   ð   ɪ   ɪ   ɪ   ɪ   ɪ
six months. We believe that your client's business is *our* business.

         ɪ   ɪ rɪ r   r
We are Universal Securities Trust—"US Trust." And we can assure

ð   ɪ
that you *will*.

CD
47

Now, mark this business pitch with any additional sounds with which you have difficulty. Then, *turn to **CD Track 47*** and listen to a recording of Fred's business pitch No. 1. Record yourself reading the pitch above, and compare your pronunciation with that on the CD track.

Fred's business pitch No. 2
(marked for the sounds *l, ʤ, b/v/w, ʌ,* and *ʊ*)

     v   l   ʊ   ʌ w   ʌ   ʤ l
Universal Securities Trust wants you to understand the generally

                 v ʊ   l   ʌ   ʌ w
enduring effect of putting together a portfolio structure underweighted

               l ʌ   ʊ   v
in a few financial companies. The good news is that moving towards

        ʌ   w l   bl   l   v lʊ
a new structure will indisputably increase cash flow. A positive outlook

  l   v bʊl   ʊ   ʤ   l
until the return of a bull market should re-energize employee

       ʌ   v   w   ʌ   ʤʌ ʌ ʌ   lʊ
productivity. We're US Trust—just trust us to look out for you!

48

Now, mark this business pitch with any additional sounds with which you have difficulty. Then, *turn to **CD Track 48*** and listen to a recording of Fred's business pitch No. 2. Record yourself reading the pitch above, and compare your pronunciation with that on the CD track.

Fred's business pitch No. 3
(marked for the sounds ð/θ, r, ŋ, e, æ, and ɔ)

> ŋ   e ð   ɔ   r   r e
> Your accounting shows a less than plausible return for projected

> re   æ   r ŋ æ   æ
> revenues, and due to a lack of operating cash flow, we cannot

> re   e ð   ɔ   æ   ɔ θ r   ŋ
> recommend that you automatically authorize complete funding

> ð   e   e   r
> on these new ventures. However, if you will allow Universal Securities

> r   ɔ   ð   ð rɔ   ɔ ð
> Trust to halt further withdrawals and overhaul these accounts

> ð   r   ɔ   æ   e r
> with a proper audit, we *can* assure you of a positive outcome. US Trust—

> r
> trust us!

49

Now, mark this business pitch with any additional sounds with which you have difficulty. Then, *turn to **CD Track 49*** and listen to a recording of Fred's business pitch No. 3. Record yourself reading the pitch above, and compare your pronunciation with that on the CD track.

Step 2: Marking operative and inoperative words

Now, we'll mark the same three business pitches for operative and inoperative words. To better highlight the images in the pitches, we'll also bracket the phrases and clauses.

Fred's business pitch No. 1

~~The~~ [following PowerPoint presentation] ~~on your~~ [computer screen] [focuses ~~on~~ creating ~~a~~ different portfolio scenario] ~~for your~~ [client's dividends]. [~~It is~~ examined] [using ~~an~~ economic deceleration model], as [delineated ~~on the~~ accompanying spreadsheets]. [~~In our~~ opinion], ~~your~~ [client's company stock dividends] ~~will be~~ [impacted] ~~and~~ [increase dramatically] ~~if this~~ [portfolio structure] ~~is~~ [implemented] ~~in the~~ [next six months]. ~~We~~ [believe] ~~that your~~ [client's business] ~~is~~ [*our* business]. ~~We are~~ [Universal Securities Trust]—["US Trust"]. ~~And we can~~ [assure ~~that you~~ *will*].

Fred's business pitch No. 2

[Universal Securities Trust] [wants ~~you to~~ understand] ~~the~~ [generally enduring effect] ~~of~~ [putting together ~~a~~ portfolio structure] [underweighted] ~~in a~~ [few financial companies]. ~~The~~ [good news] ~~is that~~ [moving ~~towards a~~ new structure] ~~will~~ [indisputably increase cash flow]. A [positive outlook] ~~until the~~ [return ~~of a~~ bull market] ~~should~~ [re-energize employee productivity]. ~~We're~~ [US Trust]— [just trust us ~~to~~ look out ~~for you~~]!

Fred's business pitch No. 3

[~~Your~~ accounting] [shows ~~a~~ less ~~than~~ plausible return] ~~for~~ [projected revenues], ~~and~~ [due ~~to a~~ lack ~~of~~ operating cash flow], ~~we~~ [cannot recommend] ~~that you~~ [automatically authorize complete funding] ~~on these~~ [new ventures]. However, ~~if you will~~ [allow Universal Securities Trust] ~~to~~ [halt further withdrawals] ~~and~~ [overhaul ~~these~~ accounts] ~~with a~~ [proper audit], ~~we~~ [*can* assure] ~~you of a~~ [positive outcome]. [US Trust]—[trust us]!

Further practice

Now, let's work on the more advanced business presentations below. After you have practiced with these sample presentations, you can apply the same steps to your own business text.

Business sample No. 1: The impact of the economic crisis on insurance companies

Begin by marking all of your difficult sounds in the paragraphs below. Underline the consonant and vowel sounds that you find challenging, then mark their phonetic symbol equivalents above.

The first text is scored for operative and inoperative words. Phrases and clauses are bracketed to highlight the desired imaging of the speaker.

[Most insurers] ~~have~~ [suffered ~~the~~ impact] ~~of~~ [depressed equity prices] ~~and of~~ [low long-term yields]. ~~Even the~~ [best-prepared companies] ~~have had to~~ [reinforce ~~their~~ hedging strategies] ~~and are~~ [currently dealing] ~~with~~ [unprecedented volatility ~~in their~~ stock prices]. ~~We are~~ [still ~~in a~~ phase] ~~where~~ [volatility ~~is~~ largely driven] ~~by the~~ [market's fears regarding solvency].

~~But~~ [looking beyond] ~~the~~ [immediate market volatility], ~~it is~~ [clear] ~~that there is~~ ["real economy" damage]. ~~This is~~ [already starting ~~to have an~~ impact] ~~on the~~ [insurance industry]. ~~We can~~ [predict ~~with~~ some certainty] ~~that~~ [customer demand] ~~will~~ [decline sharply]. [Insurers] ~~will~~ [need ~~to be~~ clear] ~~about the~~ [markets] ~~and~~ [product areas] ~~that will~~ [continue ~~to~~ thrive] ~~and that~~ [deserve strong investment], ~~those that will~~ [decline temporarily], ~~and those that~~ [present ~~an~~

opportunity] ~~for~~ [long-term share gains] ~~in~~ [exchange] ~~for~~ [short-term pain].

[Recessions] [always create opportunities] to [reshape ~~the~~ competitive landscape]. ~~The~~ [insurance industry] ~~is~~ [generally better prepared] [this time around]. ~~But the~~ [double impact] ~~of the~~ [financial crisis] ~~and the~~ [damage ~~on~~ consumer demand] mean ~~that~~ [this downturn] ~~will be~~ [no exception].

*Now listen to **CD Track 50**.* The speaker is a native of Thailand, and there are two recordings—"before" and "after" versions of Business sample No. 1. The second recording was made after learning and using the *Perfecting Your English Pronunciation* method.

Business sample No. 2: Strategy in the information systems business

Begin by marking all of your difficult sounds in the paragraph below. Underline the consonant and vowel sounds that you find challenging, then mark their phonetic symbol equivalents above.

Next, score this second text for operative and inoperative words, and bracket phrases and clauses to highlight the desired imaging of the speaker.

Let's focus on the information systems business. The issues are real.

Our company can leverage a powerful mix of technologies for the information systems. Yet other subsidiary companies—parts suppliers, electronics companies, content providers, and airtime providers— are all fighting for dominant positions in the same space. Major growth in information systems is certain—who will capture that growth is not at all clear. For our company, the information systems business represents a wonderful opportunity amidst great uncertainty and change. In the end, we must together define the core value at which our company excels, the currency that will cause partners to sign up for this integrated business model to serve the consumer. To speed our company's race towards the marketplace, and to more clearly define a strategy, we will use external interviews, internal interviews, and objective data to establish the value that each type of player brings at positions along the value chain.

*Now listen to **CD Track 51.*** The speaker is of Hispanic descent, and there are two recordings—"before" and "after" versions of Business sample No. 2. The second recording was made after learning and using the *Perfecting Your English Pronunciation* method.

Business sample No. 3: Valuation financial model

Begin by marking all of your difficult sounds in the paragraphs below. Underline the consonant and vowel sounds that you find challenging, then mark their phonetic symbol equivalents above.

Next, score this third text for operative and inoperative words, and bracket phrases and clauses to highlight the desired imaging of the speaker.

This model is a vehicle for comparing the results of your company's valuation methodology with the historical share prices of other companies under analysis. Previously, viewing the effect on share price tracking was laborious and time-consuming. Now, using this tool, your company can perform this analysis quickly. This model also allows analysis on an unlimited number of departments simultaneously, rather than one by one.

It is important to note that this model is designed for use with financial services companies. Thus, the growth rates used to create spot valuations are those of equity, not assets, and the return measure is return on equity, not return on investment. Adapting the model for use with industrial companies should not be difficult, but in its present incarnation, it applies to banks.

CD
52

*Now listen to **CD Track 52**. The speaker is a native of India, and there are two recordings—"before" and "after" versions of Business sample No. 3. The second recording was made after learning and using the *Perfecting Your English Pronunciation* method.

Scoring your presentations

You can use the following system to score all your presentations.

Step one

To "zero in on" your pronunciation problems, mark all of your difficult sounds on the presentation. If you are not certain which vowel sounds to choose, check the spelling patterns and word lists in Chapters Three through Sixteen. Underline the consonant and vowel sounds that you find challenging, then mark their phonetic symbol equivalents above.

Step two

Underline the operative words in the presentation and cross out the inoperative words. Read only the operative words. Notice that they make sense on their own; this will enable you to bracket the images. Now, bracket phrases and clauses to highlight your desired imaging.

Step three

Read the presentation once again, adding the inoperative words. This not only dramatically improves your intonation, it makes your thoughts much clearer to your listeners.

Always remember: Try to relax. Most people speak much more quickly when nervous. This was an ongoing problem for Fred, but he found that bracketing his thoughts on paper helped him slow down and let the images resonate with his audience.

Fred, by the way, is a composite of all students who have used the *Perfecting Your English Pronunciation* method. The name stands for **FR**ustrated with **E**nglish **D**iction. Fred is *you*. And Fred is frustrated no longer!

Prefixes, suffixes, and common word endings with ɪ

As indicated in Chapter Nine, the vowel ɪ is generally spelled with *i* or *y*. There are exceptions, however. When the letter *e* is used in the unstressed first syllable of a word (often a prefix like *de-, ex-,* and *re-*), it is pronounced ɪ. Following are common words that use the ɪ sound in this way.

PREFIX ɪ WITH *e* SPELLING PATTERN

because	emerge	reform
become	enjoy	release
before	exposed	relief
began	express	response
debate	extend	result
decide	extent	resume
declare	extreme	retain
decline	precise	retire
defeat	prefer	return
describe	prepare	reveal
design	receive	review
desire	reduce	select
effect	refer	
elect	reflect	

In addition, there are seven suffixes and other common word endings that use the ɪ vowel but are not spelled with *i*: *-age, -ate* (as a noun or adjective, but not as a verb), *-ed, -es, -ess, -est,* and *-et*. Following are common words that use these suffixes and common word endings.

SUFFIX *-age*

advant<u>age</u>	dam<u>age</u>	pack<u>age</u>
aver<u>age</u>	encour<u>age</u>	pass<u>age</u>
bever<u>age</u>	im<u>age</u>	percent<u>age</u>
carri<u>age</u>	langu<u>age</u>	sav<u>age</u>
cott<u>age</u>	man<u>age</u>	sew<u>age</u>
cour<u>age</u>	marri<u>age</u>	stor<u>age</u>
cover<u>age</u>	mess<u>age</u>	vill<u>age</u>

SUFFIX *-ate*

accur<u>ate</u>	doctor<u>ate</u>
adequ<u>ate</u>	elabor<u>ate</u> (*adjective*)
appropri<u>ate</u> (*adjective*)	estim<u>ate</u> (*noun*)
approxim<u>ate</u> (*adjective*)	fortun<u>ate</u>
articul<u>ate</u> (*adjective*)	gradu<u>ate</u> (*noun, adjective*)
associ<u>ate</u> (*noun, adjective*)	illegitim<u>ate</u>
candid<u>ate</u>*	immedi<u>ate</u>
clim<u>ate</u>	intim<u>ate</u> (*noun, adjective*)
corpor<u>ate</u>	legitim<u>ate</u> (*adjective*)
deliber<u>ate</u> (*adjective*)	moder<u>ate</u> (*noun, adjective*)
delic<u>ate</u>	separ<u>ate</u> (*adjective*)
desper<u>ate</u>	ultim<u>ate</u>

SUFFIX *-ed*

add<u>ed</u>	nodd<u>ed</u>	shout<u>ed</u>
grant<u>ed</u>	not<u>ed</u>	sound<u>ed</u>
greet<u>ed</u>	paint<u>ed</u>	start<u>ed</u>
guid<u>ed</u>	point<u>ed</u>	stat<u>ed</u>
hand<u>ed</u>	print<u>ed</u>	treat<u>ed</u>
hundr<u>ed</u>	quot<u>ed</u>	vot<u>ed</u>
lift<u>ed</u>	sacr<u>ed</u>	wait<u>ed</u>
need<u>ed</u>	seat<u>ed</u>	want<u>ed</u>

*The *a* of the suffix of this word may also be pronounced eĭ.

SUFFIX -*es*

blesses	lashes	passes
causes	misses	thrashes
dresses	noses	wishes

SUFFIX -*ess*

business	happiness	regardless
consciousness	helpless	stillness
darkness	illness	thickness
endless	reckless	weakness

SUFFIX -*est*

biggest	honest	modest
greatest	interest	nearest
forest	latest	prettiest
highest	longest	strongest

SUFFIX -*et*

blanket	jacket	quiet
budget	market	secret
bullet	planet	target
cricket	pocket	ticket
diet	poet	

Pronunciation of final *s*: *s* or *z*?

Nonnative speakers of English are often confused about how to pronounce the letter *s*: as a voiceless s or as a voiced z? Unfortunately, *s* can be either voiceless or voiced, independent of spelling patterns. However, there are three instances in English in which *s* is added to an existing word.

> To make a noun plural
> To make a noun possessive
> To make the third-person singular form of a present-tense verb

In these three instances, a simple rule dictates whether the *s* is voiceless or voiced. When adding *s,* look at the sound that precedes it. If the sound is voiceless, the *s* is voiceless; if the sound is voiced, the *s* is voiced.

Note, however, that if the word ends in a sibilant (s, z, ʃ, ʒ, ʧ, or ʤ), whether voiced or voiceless, the suffix is -*es* (or '*s* for possessives) and is pronounced ɪz.

Examples

Many team**s** compete, but not all win pennant**s**.

Kirk'**s** dog is ten year**s** old. Anne'**s** is still a puppy.

After Matt work**s** out at the gym, he run**s** a mile.

Fred wishe**s** that Thomas'**s** speeche**s** were shorter.

APPENDIX C

CD contents by track

CD track numbers and titles are followed by corresponding book page numbers.